Spooky Hu

Marianna Boncek

Schiffer Publishing Ltd®

4880 Lower Valley Road, Atglen, Pennsylvania 19310

Other Schiffer Books on Related Subjects
Hudson Valley Haunts: Historic Driving Tours, 978-0-7643-3173-2, $16.99
Haunted Finger Lakes, 978-0-7643-3358-3, $14.99
Haunted Rochester, 978-0-7643-3208-1, $14.99
Spirits and Death in Niagara, 978-0-7643-2965-4, $14.99

Designed by "Sue"
Type set in Bard/NewsGoth BT

ISBN: 978-0-7643-3384-2
Printed in the United States of America

Schiffer Books are available at special discounts for bulk purchases for sales
promotions or premiums. Special editions, including personalized covers, corporate
imprints, and excerpts can bwwe created in large quantities for special needs.
For more information contact the publisher:

Published by Schiffer Publishing Ltd.
4880 Lower Valley Road
Atglen, PA 19310
Phone: (610) 593-1777; Fax: (610) 593-2002
E-mail: Info@schifferbooks.com

For the largest selection of fine reference books on this and related
subjects, please visit our web site at: **www.schifferbooks.com**
We are always looking for people to write books on new and related subjects.
If you have an idea for a book please contact us at the above address.

This book may be purchased from the publisher.
Include $5.00 for shipping.
Please try your bookstore first.
You may write for a free catalog.

In Europe, Schiffer books are distributed by
Bushwood Books
6 Marksbury Ave.
Kew Gardens
Surrey TW9 4JF England
Phone: 44 (0) 20 8392 8585; Fax: 44 (0) 20 8392 9876
E-mail: info@bushwoodbooks.co.uk
Website: www.bushwoodbooks.co.uk

Contents

Dedication

For Liz and Rachel, my two luminaries,
and Hera, who has always been there for me

Acknowledgments

The ghost hunt continues. If you have visited any haunted sites in the Hudson Valley and want to share your scary stories, please do not hesitate to contact me in care of Schiffer Books or by email at mariannaboncek@ yahoo.com. In the meantime, I gratefully thank the following people for their help, support, and encouragement—this book would not have been possible without them:

† *Holley Boncek*, my brother, who is a walking encyclopedia of historical information;
† Historian *Anna Gordon*, town of Esopus;
† *Ann Linden*, Amenia Historical Society;
† Historian *Karlyn Knaust Elia*, town of Ulster;
† *Thomas Wysmuller*, New Netherlands Museum;
† *Alan Strauber*, Calvert Vaux Preservation Alliance;
† *Gregory Sokaris*, Wilderstein Historic Site;
† *Ethan P. Jackman*, Historian, Town of Lloyd;
† *Elizabeth Tartaglia and Jason Adams*, Bardavon Theater;
† *Olive Doty*, Historian, Pleasant Valley;
† *Poughkeepsie Paranormal Research Group*;
† *Pat Hall*, Old Dutch Church;
† *Christina Hope*, Marist College;
† *Brandon Pendergast and Susan Stessin-Cohn*, Historic Huguenot Street;
† *Cheryl Rice*, my friend and personal editor;
† The woman and two men who pushed my car out of the snowy ditch in front of Salisbury Manor;
† *Dinah Roseberry*, who first believed I could do this;
† Lastly, I owe a debt of gratitude to *everyone* who told me their stories.

Tracking the Ghosts

Writing about Ghosts should be easy, right?

A few years ago, I was at a paranormal conference in Gettysburg, Pennsylvania, one of the most haunted places in the United States, if not the world. I was in the sales room, looking at books, when I saw Dinah Roseberry sitting at a table with a sign that read "Author's Wanted." I had always enjoyed writing plus I was a paranormal investigator, so I thought, "How hard could this be?" I walked up to the table, introduced myself, and told Dinah I could write a book for her. She believed me. A few days later, I received the contract for what would become this book.

By day, I am a mild-mannered high school English teacher. I definitely dress the part, too: sensible shoes, comfortable clothes, reading glasses on the end of my nose. However, what most people do not know is that I am also a practicing astrologer and a sense medium. Yes, I read the stars and talk to dead people — and I am a member of a paranormal investigative organization, a dedicated group of individuals who volunteer their time to investigate hauntings up and down the Hudson Valley. My job in the group is to communicate with the haunted energies and move them on in their journey.

What I wanted this book to be was a chance for people to experience a little of what I experience as a paranormal investigator. After all, everyone loves a good ghost story. Real ghosts are even better. For this book, I decided to choose places based on their availability to the public. I wanted people not only to be able to visit the haunted places, but to also see and feel the haunted energy for themselves. What I didn't expect is that people would become so closed mouth. With few exceptions, people would tell me the long, detailed history of these places, but then would clam up when the subject of ghosts came up. It took a lot of prodding and promising their names would not be published next to the stories to get them to open up and, usually in hushed tones, tell me the ghost stories. However, once they began to talk, they all felt a sense of release being able to share the "forbidden history" of places they knew and loved.

What I also learned is that although the ghosts may be real, the stories surrounding them may not always be. I would often be told the ghost of "so-and-so" inhabited a certain place only to learn later that "so-and-so" had never actually visited the place, let alone haunt it. So, I found myself in a dilemma. Do I share with my audience the stories that may not be true or do I just talk about my encounters with haunted energies? I decided to do both and allow you, on your visits, to determine the type of haunted energy inhabiting a place. This book, while about ghost hunting, is also about having fun and connecting with "haunted history." Enjoy your visits to these places; learn their history, have fun, and hopefully, you'll see a ghost.

Most of the information in this book is from oral histories of people who asked to remain anonymous. If they have not, I have included their names along with their stories.

Using this Book

This book has been written as a tour of the Hudson Valley. You may follow the places listed here in order or you may choose a single place to spend an afternoon visiting. Though the book starts on the west side of the river and travels northward, there is no special sequence for you to follow. You may want to start with the haunted place nearest you or the one that sounds most interesting, but I suggest that you don't try to visit too many places in one day.

If you are serious about ghost hunting, plan your visit. Visit the website of the haunted site, if available. Use the website, www.mapquest.com, or your GPS to plan your visit. Buy a good map or atlas. You should always have a map with you in case you get lost. Jimapco sells an excellent map book called *Hudson Valley Street Atlas.* You can purchase a copy at the local Barnes and Noble or online at www.jimapco.com.

You can also visit these places just for the fun of visiting them and re-telling the haunted stories. The most important thing to know is that it you do not have to believe in ghosts to visit haunted places and enjoy the experience. Many people who shared their stories for this book do not believe in ghosts, yet telling ghost stories and visiting haunted places can be a fun way to spend the day with family or friends. So, I encourage you to tell each other's stories, visit these places, and continue to pass on our haunted history.

Part One:

Ghost Hunting

Chapter One

Reasons for a Haunting

Why Are Places Haunted?

There are many theories as to why places become haunted. Some places become haunted after a traumatic event. Other places are haunted by deceased owners. However, even new homes and buildings can be haunted. What all haunted places have in common is that they seem to be able to "collect" energy and it is this energy that psychics, sensitives, and mediums can feel in these haunted places. Ordinary people often can feel the energy, too. Have you ever had a "cold chill" upon entering a room or feel the hair stand up on your neck—that is what sensitives feel when they are around haunted energy.

Energy collects in a place when people leave behind emotion. A sudden or traumatic event can leave behind human emotional energy. This explains why murder sites, battlefields, and scenes of terrible accidents are often

haunted. It also explains why cemeteries are haunted. Cemeteries are sites of tremendous amount of human emotion in the form of grief. These hauntings are specific to the place that an event occurred. Oftentimes, hauntings can be in the form of spirits repeating the same action over and over again. This is referred to as an *imprint*. During an imprint, the spirit repeats the same action, often at the same time of the day. Everyone has heard stories of the haunted footsteps at the same time each night. That is an imprint—the energy repeating the same action. Imprints also explain how a single person can haunt several places. According to all the stories I have heard, it appears that Aaron Burr and "Mad" Anthony Wayne haunt several places in the Hudson Valley. Their hauntings are not the actually individual sentient spirit; rather, it is an impression these men left in the places they visited. An imprint is not a sentient spirit. A *sentient spirit* may move about and interact with people in the room. The spirit in an imprint will not attempt to communicate with anyone. An imprint is like an old-fashion record with a skip.

In other hauntings, the spirit seems to be sentient. The spirit will make noises, respond to requests, or make eye contact. In my experience, sentient spirits haunt a place for a reason. They may have a message or information they are trying to convey.

Some hauntings, though, are not visible to the human eye. In many places, you get a feeling of heaviness, a sudden chill, or a feeling of being watched. A person may hear faint, distinct music, smell cigar smoke or perfume, or even feel as if someone had touched them. These types of experiences can also be caused by "haunted energies."

Not all hauntings are negative. Places a person deeply loved or had positive experiences at can also be haunted. This explains why previous owners often haunt homes. Many times homeowners have told me that they get a feeling a spirit is sticking around to "watch over things." This also explains why places such as theaters, shopping centers, and churches can be haunted. Remember, with spirits that haunt a particular place, even though the place itself might be changed, renovated, or torn down, the spirit, sometimes, will stay. I remember seeing the spirit of a young girl on the side of the road outside of Rosendale, New York. Upon investigating, I came to believe she had lived in a home in the area, but which had been torn down decades earlier.

How does a new place become haunted? Sometimes new places are built on grounds where previous human emotional events have occurred. I investigated a haunted house in Dutchess County that was unknowingly built on a 300-year-old graveyard! Unwittingly, the owners moved into a "new" — but *haunted* — house. Luckily, we were able to convince the most bothersome spirits to move along. There can also be "restless spirits" that become attached to new places, attracted by the new energy in the new building. These energies have no "place." They are just opportunistic or even "lost" spirits. That is why sometimes "playing" with the paranormal — such as with Ouija boards and through séances — is not the best thing, especially if you have no idea what you are doing. *You can invite a spirit in and then the spirit becomes attached to this new place.* There are also hauntings that actually are not hauntings in the traditional sense; they are not people who have died. There are poltergeist activities associated with adolescents, shadow people, and other types of disincarnate spirits who have never inhabited live bodies. Energy becomes attracted to a place where it can manifest. Paranormal investigators refer to any physical signs of spirit activity — an apparition, a sound, or movement — as "manifesting."

Sometimes it seems a spirit can follow a certain individual or even a family. Wherever that person moves to, there seems to be some sort of paranormal activity. As I said, energy becomes attracted to places where it can manifest. Often times, people will allow certain kinds of energies to manifest. As a sense medium, I allow spirits to communicate with me. However, I make it clear that those energies have two choices; they may move on in their journey "to the light" (which I strongly encourage) or they can stay where they are. They may *not* come home with me. A friend of mine who visited a building, which had been used as an orphanage in the early 1890s, was a sense medium, but very new at it. He felt so moved by the spirits of the orphans, because he, too, had been an orphan, he told them they could come with him not realizing the spirits would take him at his word. After arriving home, all sorts of strange knockings on walls and doors started to happen around his house.

People can be the vehicle that allows energies to manifest in their environment. The good news is that once a person becomes aware that he/she is allowing this energy to manifest, there are easy steps that can be taken to stop the hauntings. The quickest way is to tell the haunted energy it is no longer welcome and should move into the light. When I find a haunting attached to a person, it is usually because the person is giving the haunting too much attention, which is energy, and thereby allowing the energy to manifest.

I used to live in a large farmhouse in Sullivan County, New York, that was haunted by a dog. (Yes, ghosts can be animals, too.) The first night in our new home, we heard a whining in the basement. We carefully searched the empty basement and could find no source of the whining. On and off, the dog would continue to whine in the basement. One day, while I was writing, I was feeling particularly stressed because I had a deadline, but I was nowhere near finished with my project. I heard a dog whining, and not thinking about ghosts, thought it was my own big black lab, Rosie. I got up to let Rosie outside only to find her fast asleep under the dining room table. It was not Rosie, but our ghost dog. No sooner had I started typing again, the ghost dog started to whine. I went to the top of the basement stairs and called down, "lie down and go to sleep!" just like I would have with my own dog if she was begging for attention. The dog stopped whining and I was able to get my work done. Once our ghost dog realized we were going to treat him just like a member of the family and not give him any special attention he moved on. We did not hear from him again.

As you can see, there are many reasons why a haunting may occur — and just as many places to find them. The kind of energy that can produce a haunting can be found almost anywhere. So, even though the places in this book are "guaranteed haunted," it doesn't mean you can't find places on your own for ghost hunting. Just make sure you leave the ghosts behind when you leave.

Visiting Haunted Places

Visiting haunted places can be a fun way to spend an afternoon with either your family or a group of ghost hunting friends. However, I have seen too many important, historic places vandalized by people claiming to be looking for ghosts. If we are considerate and respectful of the historic and metaphysical places we visit, they will be preserved for future generations of ghost hunters. Here is a list of suggestions for visiting haunted places:

1. **DO NOT TRESPASS**. Many of the places listed in this book are open to the public. Observe the times and rules for entry. Please listen to the guides who are available in many of the historic places. For those places *not* open to the public, do not trespass. If it's listed here, it is either open to the public or observable from public property. You must stay on public property. Please respect the privacy of others.

2. **BE RESPECTFUL**. Many haunted sites are also historic sites. The only souvenirs you should take home with you are pictures and EVP recordings. When visiting cemeteries, please remember these are the final resting places of loved ones. Do not talk loudly, laugh, or walk on the graves. Do not let children run around or bring pets. If allowed, you may take pictures and voice recordings. Do so as discreetly as you can. Respect people visiting loved ones. If there is a funeral in progress, wait until the funeral is over before continuing your visit. Believe it or not, graveyards are not always safe places to visit and it has nothing to do with ghosts. Never visit a graveyard alone. Never visit a graveyard after dark unless you have written permission from the governing agency. If there seems to be suspicious people in the graveyard, leave immediately.

3. **BRING YOUR OWN FOOD**. Bring snacks with you. Most of the places listed here do not sell food or drink; if they do, they may only do so in the summertime. I suggest bringing snacks with you from the get-go, so that you won't have to stop a hunt to make a jaunt to the store. I get so involved with ghost hunting I hate to have to stop and drive to get supplies. But remember the "carry in, carry out rule." Do not litter.

4. **DRESS APPROPRIATELY.** The Hudson region can be very hot and humid in the summer months and bitterly cold in the winter. Most of these places are best visited in good weather like the spring or fall. In the summer, bring sunscreen, mosquito repellant, and a hat. In the winter, make sure your head and hands are covered and you have warm socks. No matter what the season wear layers and good walking shoes. You will be walking quite a bit to see these sites.

5. **BRING EQUIPMENT**. Bring any equipment you plan to use, such as cameras, voice recorders, and camcorders. I have a special "ghost bag" that I keep stocked and ready to go at a moment's notice; it contains my camera, a digital recorder, an EMF reader, a journal, pens, chargers for all my equipment, plenty of extra batteries, and my map book. Remember, however, you must observe the rules posted at all sites. Some places do not allow you to take photographs indoors. The notebook is to record your pictures, impressions, and findings while they are still fresh in your mind. Ask guides about ghosts.

6. **OBSERVE YOUR SURROUNDINGS**. Allow yourself to experience what the site offers. Do not go with expectations. You may encounter a ghost and you may not. Sometimes, you will have to visit a site several times to get a "feel" for it before being able to sense a ghost. I know a ghost hunter with decades of experience—yet he has *never* experienced an apparition. However, he has taken some amazing pictures and EVPs. Don't give up. It will be worth it!

7. **KEEP A JOURNAL**. You may eventually get your favorite ghost hunting spots. By keeping a journal, you will find where you have the best experiences and where you have taken the best photographs and EVPs. I have a friend who has visited his favorite spot hundreds of time and has never comes home disappointed.

8. **ENJOY**. Most importantly, enjoy what you are doing. Someday you may contribute to the field of paranormal investigations. Even if you don't, you can still enjoy a rewarding hobby.

Chapter Two:

Gathering Your Evidence

Orb Phenomena

An *orb* is a spherical body, usually transparent, that can show up in pictures. While mostly translucent, orbs can appear in a wide variety of colors, such as, red, yellow, orange, and purple.

There are many natural causes of orb phenomena: dust, rain, and external lighting. However, it is my experience that not all orbs are caused by natural phenomena. Some seem to be related to paranormal activity. When I take "regular" pictures, such as family gatherings, special occasions, or events, I never get a picture of an orb. The only time I have photographed an orb is when I have been on a paranormal investigation. Therefore, I tend to believe that the orb phenomena suggest paranormal activity. Whether you believe in the orb phenomena or not (and I encourage you to investigate on your own), it's fun trying to "capture" an orb picture when you're visiting haunted places. If you're lucky, not only will you get a picture of an orb, but also you will get a picture of a mist, which some paranormal investigators refer to as "ectoplasm" or it's shorten form, "ecto." Technically, this mist is not ectoplasm.

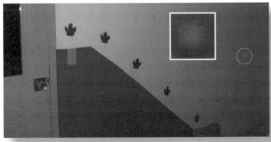

Small orb (circled) joins me during a ghost hunt on a haunted staircase. Inset: Detail of orb.

Another orb (circled) joins me on the haunted staircase. Inset: Detail of orb.

Ectoplasm, by definition, is a physical manifestation, usually in a gel form, of a paranormal event. Ectoplasm manifestations were a popular phenomenon in the late 1800s—and were mostly faked. However, some haunted places do report ectoplasm, usually seeping out of walls. Chances are you won't get a picture of ectoplasm, but you may very well get a picture of a ghostly mist. It is important to note that mists you capture in ghost photography are usually not visible to the human eye. You will only be able to see it after you view the pictures you have taken.

Orbs can show up anywhere. When investigating, take pictures everywhere. However, it has also been my experience that you can actually get more pictures of orbs when you express the intention that you would like to see an orb in your photographs. I remember one particular investigation I spent the whole night taking pictures. I took several hundred pictures and not one orb showed up. The other investigators, who were photographing right along with me, were able to capture many orbs. I finally said aloud, "I'd really like to get a picture of you." My next several pictures had clear and definite orbs.

Photographing Orb and Mist Phenomena

1. **Take many pictures**. Take them in mundane places, hallways, entryways... any room or space where many "living" people have passed. Remember, the more "live" energy deposited in an area the better chance there is spirit activity in that area as well. Do not delete any pictures on your digital camera until you have downloaded and reviewed them on a larger screen. Orbs can be very small or faint and not noticeable until you download them.

2. **Express your intention out loud**. Say that you want to photograph an orb. It may sound silly, but I have found it works. A simple statement such as "I'd really like to have a picture of you before I leave" can work. An investigator I know uses this technique graveyards; he moves slowly from grave to grave, carefully reading aloud from the gravestone. A partner will snap photographs as he does this.

3. **Don't give up!** It *will* happen. Of course, the place you are visiting must be haunted to get haunted pictures. Just don't give up.

4. **Is it really an orb?** Orbs can also be caused by lighting, dust, and moisture.If suddenly, you get dozens of orbs in your picture, someone in your ghost hunting party has kicked up dust or it has started to rain. Experience will tell you if you have a ghost orb or something else.

5. **"Following" the Orb**. If everyone is snapping pictures together or you are videotaping, you can actually follow the path of your orbs. It's exciting to "see" its path as it shoots across a room or out a door. You'll want to keep a photo album to have a record of the place, time, and date of your orbs.

Electronic Voice Phenomena

Electronic Voice Phenomena, or EVP, is the recording of unknown voices onto a voice recorder. Most investigators believe that these voices are spirit voices. EVPs can provide some of the most compelling—*and creepiest*—evidence in paranormal investigation. Like photographing orbs, it may take some time to start recording EVPs. I have known investigators to place their recording devices side by side and one investigator will record a voice and the other one record nothing. If you are good with technological devices, you can research on the Internet and find advanced ways to capture EVPs. There are even groups that give training sessions on how to capture an EVP. Those advanced techniques are more for the serious ghost hunter and not the weekend kind. However, these steps below are for the novice who would like to give voice recording a try.

1. **Any recorder will do**. You do not have to invest a lot of money. You may use a recorder you already have.
2. **Know how to work your recorder**. You want to know how to record, rewind, replay, and avoid erasing. You do not want to be fumbling around with your recorder at the site or accidentally delete recordings. Remember, you can get EVPs just about anywhere. However, you should limit your recording to the amount you are willing to process by listening. A half an hour is a good amount of time for beginners. The ghost shows on television are glamorous, but oftentimes, to get one good EVP word or phrase, you will spend hours and hours taping and listening.
3. **A quiet place is best**. You do not want a lot of outside noise obstructing the spirit voices. However, one of the best EVPs I have heard recorded was while I was interviewing a homeowner of a haunted house. I asked the question, "Does the ghost bother you?" The homeowner replied, "No," but a distinct voice was heard saying in the background, "We will now." If you can place the recorder and move out of the area, that is even better. That way you will not accidentally get one of your party's voices and mistake it for a spirit voice. In a graveyard, you can leave your recorder by a grave while you visit the rest of the graveyard. To avoid detection, you can put it behind a plant or some other item so other visitors will not detect it.
   A very good technique is to sit quietly and ask questions. Give time between questions for a response (1-2 minutes). You may ask questions like, "Is anyone here?" "Do you have anything you'd like to say?" Or "Who are you?" You should write out a list of questions beforehand. Keep them short and simple. This technique makes playback and listening easier because you only have to listen between questions at shorter intervals.

4. **Record the time and day**. Before beginning your recording session, announce the time, date, and place for future reference. When you end the session, you should say something like "End session" and give time and date.

5. **Don't expect a clear, sharp voice**. When you start getting voices, they may sound mechanical and hard to understand. You may get a single garbled or indiscriminate word. A friend of mine got one voice just saying the word "apple." Do not be discouraged. Those great recordings you hear on websites and TV are one in hundreds, if not thousands, of recordings by a single investigator.

6. **The Headphones**. Purchase "sound canceling" headphones for listening. You may need to turn up the volume on your recorder to be able to hear.

7. **Be prepared for "malfunctions."** Do not be upset if your recording device "malfunctions" or turns itself off. This has been a very common experience in my paranormal investigations. Remember, you will not hear the voices until you play the recording back. However, some recorders have a light that lights up when they are recording sound. This may indicate to you that you have a voice.

8. **Be patient**. Some people have to try regularly for months before they get their first audible word.

If you are interested, there are computer programs that will actually show a visual "peak" when something is recorded so you can focus on that part of the recording. Again, for people who are good at using technical devices, there are all sorts of software programs that can be used to listen to the voices. Do a web search on "electronic voice phenomenon." But do not be surprised if you get hooked on this fascinating part of paranormal investigations.

Chapter Three:

Haunted Hudson Valley

Just Their Names Sends Shivers

Haunted Names

Some places in the Hudson Valley retain their haunted names. Just like other places, people tend to name roads, towns and other areas for a person or an event. You can visit these spooky places in the Hudson Valley:

Hessian Lake
Also known as Bloody Pond, it's located in Bear Mountain State Park. This was the scene of a bloody Revolutionary War battle. The lake was bloodied with the bodies of the Hessian soldiers who died there during an attack.

Murderers Creek
Located in Athens, it's named for a young woman found brutally murdered there. Her killer was never found.

The sign for Murderers Creek, Athens, is a reminder of the unsolved murder that happened on its shores.

Fiddler's Bridge
This bridge was named for a fiddler murdered while on his way home from a party.

Moodna Creek
From the Dutch word for "murder," it's the site of a grisly Native American murder of a colonial family that lived on its shores.

Spooky Names

Spook is a Dutch word meaning "ghost" or "specter." Many places still retain their "spooky" name. Grab a map and go see if these places are still spooky.

Spook Hill Road, Wappingers Falls
Spook Rock Road, Hudson
Spook Hollow Road, Nyack
Spook Hollow Road and Spook Field, Fishkill
Spook Bridge, Glenford
Spook Hole Road, Ellenville
Spook Rock Road, Suffern

~~~~~

The Hills and The River

The west side of the river contains the Catskill and Shawangunk (pronounced SHON-gum) Mountains. The Native Americans believed that both these mountain ranges had their own very distinct spirits and were haunted. Some early Dutch families in New Paltz settled on the east bank of the Wallkill River because they believed the west side was inhabited by werewolves. The Catskill Mountains are believed to be inhabited by a race of small, gnome-like creatures that mine ore. What type of metal they mine is unclear. Some say it is silver and there are legends about secret ores of silver in the Catskill Mountains. You will probably remember the story of Rip Van Winkle and his fateful visit with these mischievous men. Normally, I would discount a race of little people living in these hills, but I did recently hear an account by a normal, rational woman who claimed to see a "little person" standing on her back deck.

There are also stories of black, shadowlike figures called Shadow People who are said to inhabit the woody areas of the Shawangunk. Like most spirits, tradition holds they cannot cross water. That explains why they haunt the west side of the Hudson but not the east

A view of the Hudson River and mountains from Boscobel mansion in Garrison. Henry Hudson sailed up the river in 1609 in search of the North-West Passage.

Shadow People is a paranormal phenomenon of a being that resembles a shadow, hence its name. Shadow People are also called Shadow Beings or Shadow Men because they always manifest in the form of a man. There is plenty of literature about Shadow People. You can find instances of Shadow People in any culture that has lived in forested areas. The Native Americans who inhabited these hills believed in Shadow People. Shadow People are very dark, often large, human-like forms that never fully manifest, that is, never take the shape of a complete human being. They will never appear more than just a shadow. Witnesses who have experienced Shadow People, often describe them as hooded or wearing some sort of hat. Shadow People will appear at the edges of forests or in your peripheral vision. They tend to disappear as soon as a person notices them. They often bring with them a feeling of sheer dread or terror. Most people's encounters with Shadow People leave them deeply shaken often for a very long time, with many of them being able to recount the event in vivid detail years or even decades later.

Shadow People are *not* ghosts. They have never been human. Unlike ghosts, they will never manifest facial features, dress like humans or attempt to communicate, as ghosts will. If they do manifest any features, at all, it will be eyes and they are usually described as glowing orbs.

You will probably know if a Shadow Person is nearby. You will get an unexplainable creepy feeling. If you are out hiking, looking for hauntings, and get the feeling you are being watched, start snapping your pictures. Aim towards the edge of the woods. Good places to focus on are edges of the road where the trees have been cleared.

If you start to feel afraid, leave the area, make noise or sing. Remember, Shadow People will usually disappear if noticed, so *notice* them. Snapping the camera, talking, and singing are the best way to show them that you know they are there.

While I am not afraid of Shadow People, I do not enjoy my encounters with them. Its not that I feel they are dangerous, they aren't. There have been a few isolated accounts of shadow people "chasing" witnesses but I think this has to do with the sense of fear a felt by the witness. The Shadow Person is not actually chasing the witness, rather, the witness may become frighten and feel the need to flee the area. I come in contact with ghosts, all the time, while working in the field of paranormal investigations. Ghosts do not make you feel creepy (though you may feel nervous or anxious). Oftentimes, ghosts even leave people with happy feelings. However, Shadow People will never leave a person feeling good about the encounter. I have only encountered Shadow People twice during investigating haunted places. One encounter was a house in Dutchess County, New York that was built over an old cemetery. The Shadow Person lurked in the heavy, brushy woods surrounding the house. The second encounter with a Shadow Person was in the old morgue, now used as an office building. Since I knew the type of energy, I was experiencing, I wasn't frightened but neither was it a pleasant experience.

Since an encounter with Shadow People can be disturbing, I strongly suggest you do not bring children on ghost hunts where you or someone else has experienced an unexplained "creepy feeling" that would not go away or a feeling of being watched.

While Shadow People are said to inhabit any heavily forested place, each forested place seems to have its own unique type of spirts. I love the mountains and hike quite frequently, but rarely do I get any sense of being watched by a malevolent spirit. Most of the spirits here have a very uplifting feel to them. There are a few isolates spots, however, that I feeling that I am being watched. Some people say they feel no malevolent spirits in the Catskills, but more so in the Shawangunk.

Friedrich Jurgenson, considered the Father of the Electronic Voice Phenomenon, began his research accidentally. He went out into the woods to record birdsong and when he returned home, he found he had also recorded human voices, even though he had been in a remote area. So, even a day hike into these enchanted mountains can become a chance for a ghost hunt or a chance to collect some EVPs.

Chapter Four:

The River that Flows Both Ways

The Half Moon

Everyone knows Washington Irving's story of Rip Van Winkle, the man who fell asleep for one hundred years in the woods of the Catskill Mountains. Washington Irving claims, "Whoever has made a voyage up the Hudson must remember the Catskill Mountains." If you take a boat trip up the Hudson, the mountains rise from the west. No matter how many times I see these mountains, in any season, they take my breath away. Living among these mountains has given me a sense of peace and well-being. The Catskill Mountains hold a very special energy. I have no doubt that Henry Hudson's crew felt this same sense of wonder and enchantment when they saw them for the first time.

In 1609, Henry Hudson, an Englishman sailing for the Dutch East India Company, was one of the first Europeans to head up the Hudson River. He did not discover the river. John Cabot had discovered it earlier in 1498, just five years after Columbus' discovery of the "New World," and Giovanni da Verrazzano, for whom the Verrazano Narrows are named, sailed up the Hudson in 1524. Verrazzano sailed as far as the Palisades. A year later, Esteven Gomez also sailed up the Hudson. Not to mention all the Norsemen, who will forever remained unnamed, who sailed up the Hudson long before Columbus arrived. But it was Henry Hudson who was first to explore its beautiful shores and his are the first European's recollections and myths we have. He was in search of the north-west passage, a "short cut" to the Far East. It is said that members of Hudson's ship, the *Half Moon*, (in Dutch *De Halve Maen*), became enchanted, as if in a spell-like state, as they sailed up the river. Hudson called the river, which would later bear his name, "The River of Mountains." The Native American name for the Hudson was "Muhheakunnuk" or "The River That Flows Both Ways." Adding to the Hudson River's unique nature, the river is technically not a river at all, but an estuary of the Atlantic. Being an estuary, the Hudson is a tidal river. Therefore, it can seem that the river actually flows both ways, depending on the tides.

Henry Hudson met his demise in 1611 on another ship, aptly named the *Destiny*. His crew, tired of looking for the fabled Northwest Passage,

A view of the Hudson River from Bear Mountain State Park.

mutinied and set Hudson, his son, and some loyal crew members adrift, ironically in the bay that would later also bear his name, Hudson Bay. Hudson and his crew were never heard from again. *The Half Moon* lasted a bit longer, finally sinking in a wreck in the Indian Ocean during a journey for the Dutch East India Company.

Upon the "discovery" of the Hudson River and the native people inhabiting its shores, ghost stories started to erupt into the Dutch culture almost immediately. The local Native Americans had legends of a race of little people who worked with metals. One of the oddest stories of Henry Hudson and his crew is their meeting up with this race of "little people" on the shores of the river. These people are often referred to as the Catskill gnomes. According to this strange legend, after putting to shore for the night, Hudson heard music and he and crew members went to investigate. They happened upon men, described as pig-like with bushy beards. The little people were miners. They carried with them picks, shovels and bags tied with rope for carrying their ore. Interested in finding out what was being mined, after all, Hudson was not just a sea captain but a businessman as well, he and his men joined the little people in drinking and partying around the fire. As the night progressed, Hudson, to his horror, noticed that his own men were turning into "little people." Hudson asked the head of the "little people" what was going on and the little chieftain explained to Hudson that the grog they were drinking was enchanted and all would be fine in the morning. True to his word, though very hung over, the entire crew returned back to normal.

The legend goes on to tell us that every twenty years, from the date of the first meeting, September 3, 1609, Hudson and the "little people" can be heard partying on the shores of the Hudson River. People claim to have seen the party fire and hear the playing of ninepins, perhaps inspiring the Washington Irving story of *Rip Van Winkle*. Depending on who tells the story, the little people have been described to me as gnomes, leprechauns, dwarves, and earth sprites. They are said to still inhabit the Catskill Mountains, living in small caves or under large trees.

People have claimed, from the earliest times, spotting the *Half Moon*, in full sail, headed up the Hudson River. Reports from early Dutch settlements claim they would spot a ship, usually in the evening, in full sail headed swiftly up the Hudson, often sailing impossibly against the tide. Hails to the ship go unanswered. Witnesses who have gotten close enough to the ship have report seeing a full crew compliment—all in Dutch style clothing. Though the ship appears to have a full sailing crew, none actually seem to be sailing the ship; it seems to be sailing on its own. The crew reportedly stands silent, immobile, and unaware of anything around them.

To this day, people claim to see the *Half Moon* headed up the Hudson (never down). The ship is most often sighted in the summer or early fall, about the time of year the *Half Moon* originally headed up the Hudson. Most often, the moon is full when the ship is spotted. The ship will not "tack." Sailing ships must "tack," that is, make a zigzagging pattern to catch the wind in their sails to move them up river. The *Half Moon*, as a ghost ship, will not tack but appear to sail straight up the river, often impossibly against the tides. Sometimes it will sail quickly up the river and sometimes it will just disappear. Claims have been made that very late at night, when the river is at its quietest, you can hear the sailors singing. There are still some wonderfully uninhabited shorelines of the Hudson that are perfect for late night star gazing and listening for the singing ghost sailors.

There are many places to go "*Half Moon* hunting" along the Hudson. However, most sightings of the *Half Moon* are reported just north of Poughkeepsie at the riverfront in Hyde Park. Henry Hudson began his exploration of the river on September 2, 1609 and went as far as Albany. He then left the Hudson on October 4th of the same year. Therefore, this span, from September 2 to October 4, is the best time to go look for a "ghost ship." Remember, that Henry Hudson's ship was small in comparison to today's large modern ships. You are looking for a sailing vessel that only eighty-five feet long. Do not confuse it with *The Clearwater*, a sloop, whose purpose is to educate people about the Hudson River. The *Half Moon*, as a ghost ship, may appear and disappear quite quickly. If you don't get to catch a glimpse of the ship, remain quiet and you may hear the sailor's singing. Remember, the singing will not be in English. Even if you don't get to see the *Half Moon* this is a wonderful time of year to visit the Hudson Valley and tell ghost stories.

Finally, if you do not want to spend your nights looking for the *Half Moon*, or you want to take a look at the ship before you ghost hunt, you can see a replica of it. You may actually want to visit this ship first, if you plan to "ghost hunt" for the *Half Moon* to know what type of ship to spot. The replica of the Half Moon is a traveling museum. To find its schedule, visit the website of the New Netherland Museum at http://www.halfmoon.mus.ny.us/.

Where to look for the Half Moon

There are many places to get close to the Hudson River. You can just find your favorite spot by driving up Route 9 on the east side of the river or Route 9W on the west side of the river. A good place to picnic and spend the day right on the water is at the Mills Mansion.

One of my favorite places to go ghost hunting along the Hudson is on the west side of the river outside of Port Ewen. Follow River Road (County Route 24) just south of the village of Port Ewen. River Road follows right along the Hudson River. There are many nice areas to pull-off and a small park to have a picnic. River Road will loops back to route 9W. What is good about ghost hunting here is that you can be there after dark. You can set up cameras, your EVP equipment, and sip hot cider. An archeological dig along a stretch of River Road turned up Native American artifacts. A ghost hunter friend of mine puts it this way, "There's a lot of weird stuff happening on that road." There's only one way for you to find out if he's right!

Part Two:

East Side of the River

The source of the Hudson River is in the Adirondack Mountains. The Hudson spans 306 miles to New York City where it runs into the New York Bay. North of Rockland County to just below Albany is known as the Mid-Hudson Region. The haunted sites listed in this book are all in the Mid-Hudson region. There are several bridges to cross back and forth across the Hudson River in the Mid-Hudson region, Bear Mountain Bridge, The Newburgh-Beacon Bridge (Hamilton Fish Bridge), the Mid-Hudson Bridge (Franklin D. Roosevelt Bridge), The Kingston Rhinecliff Bridge and the Rip-Van Winkle Bridge. Crossing east to west on any bridge is free, but to cross west to east there is a fee. Route 9 runs the full length of the Mid-Hudson region on the east side of the river, 9W on the west side of the river.

Chapter Five:

Peekskill

Annsville Creek

Mouth of the Annsville Creek... Wraiths, orbs of light, and a barking white dog
wander this area looking for lost treasure

The Annsville Creek runs into the Hudson River just north of Peekskill. The Metro-North rail line spans the mouth of the Annsville Creek. According to legend, a Dutch crew hid treasure somewhere in this area. Over the years, the shoreline of the Hudson changed here due to flooding and people newly inhabiting the area. Because of this, when the crew returned, they could not find their hidden treasure. They searched relentlessly for it. They feared the locals had found their treasure and grew angry. The sailors threatened the locals and swore they would never stop searching until they found it. At low tide, when there is no moon, people say glowing wraiths appear, accompanied by a howling white hound, in search of their treasure. People have also claimed to see glowing orbs of light floating above the water.

Visiting the Annsville Creek

† Annsville Creek Paddle Center
Phone: 914-739-2588
Website: www.paddlesportcenter.com
Email: info@paddlesportcenter.com

~~~~~

† Hudson Highlands State Park, 9D Beacon
Phone: 845-225-7207
Website: http://nysparks.state.ny.us/parks/info.
    asp?parkID=130

One of the easiest ways to visit Annsville Creek is at the Annsville Creek Paddlesport Center. The Center is part of the Hudson Highlands State Park and is located at the Route 9 traffic circle between Cortlandt and Peekskill. This is a great place to park and ghost hunt. There is a very short walking trail, benches and picnic tables. The Park is open year round.

Chapter Six:

Garrison

Boscobel

Boscobel is a Neoclassical Federal style mansion on the east bank of the Hudson River opposite the United States Military Academy at West Point. I have been traveling up and down the Hudson all my life and the views at Boscobel are, by far, the most breathtaking. The house was finished in 1808 for the States Dyckman family. It took four years to build. It is considered one of the finest examples of Federal architecture in the United States. It has one of the best collections of furniture and decoration from the Federal period and is worth the historic visit to this site.

Boscobel, Garrison... The figure of a woman has been seen gazing out at the river below.

However, the mansion did not always sit on this breath-taking site. It was originally located fifteen miles south of its present sight in Montrose, New York. Yes, you read that correctly; this house was *moved* fifteen miles up the Hudson.

After the Dyckman family sold the house in the early 1900s, the house went through a series of owners. The land was finally sold to the U.S. government and a Veteran's Hospital was built on the site. In the 1950s, the U.S. Government sold the mansion for $35 to a salvage company. The salvage company began to disassemble the mansion and sold pieces of it to private collectors. Luckily, private donors, realizing the historical value of the mansion, came to its rescue and purchased it. Unbelievably, the entire mansion was taken apart, piece-by-piece, and stored. The parts sold by the salvage company were found and purchased back. In 1956 a generous, anonymous donor (later identified as Lila Acheson Wallace, co-founder of *The Reader's Digest*) provided enough money so the current location on the Hudson River could be purchased and the reassembling the house could start. It took five years to meticulously re-create the mansion on its current site (one year longer than to build the original) and it was opened on May 21, 1961.

I attended a lecture in Stattsburg, New York, given by Michael J. Worden, an investigator who works with the world famous paranormal investigator Linda Zimmerman. According to Worden, the house is haunted. There are reports of a woman gazing out one of the large front windows of the house. The woman has been seen by both people inside and outside of the house. Maybe it's Mrs. Dykes admiring her house's new view. There are other ghosts wandering around, making sure the house is well kept. The ghost of a housekeeper is thought to keep close tabs on any restoration work being done in the house. Her footsteps are thought to be the one people hear walking through the house.

It's a good place to see some of the finest examples of historic design and meet a friendly ghost or two.

Visiting Boscobel

† Boscobel, 1601 Route 9D, Garrison, NY
Phone: 845-265-3638
Website: www.boscobel.org
Email: info@boscobel.org

Boscobel is open every day except Thanksgiving and Christmas. The museum and grounds are closed to the public January, February and March.

Chapter Seven:

Carmel

Smalley Inn

Smalley Inn is one of the most famous haunted places in the Hudson Valley. Smalley is a small roadside inn in Carmel, New York, but don't let its unassuming exterior fool you. This place is one big haunted treat!

Smalley Inn also packs a lot of history. It is one of the oldest continuously operating taverns in New York State, built in the mid-1800s by James Smalley. Many paranormal investigators have investigated the inn and it is a subject of many books and articles. I have also spoken with investigators who have investigated this inn. By all accounts, this place is very haunted.

Smalley Inn, Carmel... The ghost of a murder victim and a past owner are two of the many ghosts willing to entertain you during your stay.

Vincent T. Dacquino, author of *Haunting of the Hudson River Valley: An Investigative Journey*, has extensively researched the history of Smalley and the possible causes of the hauntings. Dacquino concludes that one of the many ghosts haunting the tavern is George Denny. According to records, Denny murdered an 80-year-old man and was executed by hanging. The hanging took place just across the street. Ever since then, George has been causing mischief at Smalley.

But George isn't the inn's only ghost. According to Dacquino, as well as others I spoke with, Smalley's is quite crowded in the *ghostly* sense. The mirror above the bar is haunted. People have claimed to see all sorts of images in the mirror: odd faces, shapes, and lights. Smalley is also inhabited by the former owner's wife, Mrs. Smalley, and their daughter, Elizabeth, who both have been seen walking around the tavern. There is the ghost of a soldier, a slave, and other men and women who present themselves on a regular basis. Patrons and employees have also reported their clothes being pulled or of being poked.

This is a great place to visit and have dinner, but be sure to bring your camera. While there ask your server to tell you a ghost story. You will not be disappointed.

Visiting Smalley

† Smalley Inn, 57 Gleneida Avenue (Route 52), Carmel, New York 10512
   Phone: 845-225-9874

Chapter Eight:
Wappingers Falls

Bowdoin Park

Bowdoin Park is a 301-acre park located in the town of Poughkeepsie on the Hudson River. Archeological evidence indicates that Native Americans inhabited the land 10,000 years ago. Two Native American rock shelters still exist in the park. In the late 1600s, the Dutch arrived in the area. Standing at the top of the clearing and looking south, down the Hudson River, it is easy to see why people have inhabited this area for thousands of years. Though commercially filled in years ago, you can still see where this part of the Hudson was a natural inlet, or harbor, for docking boats.

While several parts of the park are considered haunted, most recent reports are of a little girl, about five-years-old, haunting the dirt access road. She has been seen, in broad daylight, crossing the dirt road and heading up the hill into the woods, where she promptly disappears. She is dressed in a white blouse and red shorts. The former staff member who reported this sighting has seen her twice, while driving on the road, and in the company of other witnesses. The first time he saw the girl, he stopped the car and got out, fearing it was a real little girl who had fallen or wandered away from her family. However, she simply disappeared. Both times, passengers in the car saw the same apparition.

In one of the main buildings, a haunting has created some ghostly disturbances for the maintenance staff. One night, a maintenance person, on his rounds after the park closure, noticed a light on in one of the buildings. He got out of his truck and entered the building. Because of the way the building is set up, he had to first turn off the light, then walk down a very short hallway and exit the building. He entered the building, turned off the light and as he started down the hallway, he heard footsteps on the stairs. Thinking he had just turned the lights off on a co-worker, he rushed back, turned on the lights to find no one there. He searched around and found the building empty. Again, he turned off the lights and began down the hall only again to hear the footsteps again. This time, instead of turning back, he rushed outdoors and locked the door behind him. Some time later, while headed home, he noticed the light on in the building. He parked his vehicle and approached the door. It was locked, exactly as he had left it. He decided to leave the light on.

The haunted tree at Bowdoin Park, Poughkeepsie... Legend holds that a Native American was hanged from this tree. There spirits can still be seen in the form of ghostly orbs.

I had the opportunity to investigate this site with a paranormal investigation group. During our investigation of the building, we encountered a strange occurrence. I was downstairs, alone, when I heard music and assumed it was one of the other investigator's cell phone, which she had forgotten to turn off. However, the music did not stop. Now, thinking it was one of the investigators outdoors, I opened the door only to find that no one was outside and the night was silent. I went up the stairs, to get investigators who had equipment. Most of the investigators were able to hear the music. It sounded like a radio set on a classical station. We turned on the lights, and with flashlights, looked everywhere for a possible source of this music, none was found. Every time we thought we were getting closer to the source, it seemed just off in the next room.

One of the investigators snapped a picture of a white mist on the stairs. We also had an incident of a moving chair. Every investigation begins by taking pictures of the area, in the light, so we have reference pictures. While a person takes pictures, other investigators set up equipment. Everyone agrees not to move any items during the investigation unless he or she notes it. Once the investigation began, a member, investigating the large room, noticed that there was a chair directly in front of a door, which he did not remember being there during our first "walk through." We reviewed the photographs and saw the chair had in fact been moved. We questioned all the investigators and none had moved the chair.

As a sense medium, I met all sorts of spirits on these grounds. Though I did not encounter the little girl, I did meet a Native American on the grounds; he tried to talk with me, but did not speak English. I also met a frisky ghostly collie. Not all ghosts are human. There is also a very large tree on the far side of the park that is said to be haunted. Oral history claims that some Native Americans were hanged from this tree. When investigating members of our group were able to photograph significant orb activity by this tree.

This is a great place to ghost hunt in the daytime since there has been a daytime sighting.

Visiting Bowdoin Park

† Dutchess County Bowdoin Park, 85 Sheafe Road, Wappingers Falls, New York 12590

Phone: 845-298-4600

Website: www.co.dutchess.ny.us/CountyGov/Departments/DPW-Parks/PPbowdoin.htm

Entry into the park is free. Parking is down by the Hudson, but walk around the park.

~~~~~

Rochdale

Rochdale is a hamlet on the east town line of Poughkeepsie. Wappingers Creek flows through the hamlet. The Wappinger Native Americans inhabited this area before the Dutch began to settle here. The Native Americans used this river for fishing, since the river hold a wide variety of fish species. The creek is still used today for fishing and has public access for this purpose. In the autumn, the apparition of a lovely, young Native American woman appears near the creek. She is dressed in all white buckskin and carries and infant in her arms. She is thought to be the daughter of one of the last chiefs of the area. People who have seen the apparition claim she appears wet, and distressed. Supposedly, she had been traveling on the creek, when her canoe overturned, sending her and her infant into the creek. She was able to save the infant but died in the act of saving her child. Once attracting attention, she will fall to her knees and disappear. The best time to look for her is in the early autumn, in the evening, near the water.

Visiting Rochdale

† From Poughkeepsie:

Take Route 44 to Rochdale Road. Take Titus Road, off Rochdale, and park in the public waterway access. Leave enough room for fishermen to park.

Be careful walking on this road; it is very narrow and there is no shoulder. Rochdale Road loops back to Route 44.

Chapter Nine:

Poughkeepsie

Vassar College

Matthew Vassar founded Vassar College in 1861 as a women's college. Tradition holds that the main building was designed so it could easily be converted into a brewery if the college did not succeed. However, the college did succeed and quickly earned a reputation of one of the finest learning institution in the United States for women. Vassar opened its doors to men in 1969. The buildings of Vassar College are architecturally pleasing. Its grounds are gracious and visits in the summer will greet you with well-tended flower gardens, verdant lawns and fine architecture.

Main Building of Vassar College, Poughkeepsie... Ghostly girls open doors and walk through walls in the Main Building.

Matthew Vassar, founder of Vassar College, is still seen walking around the campus and overseeing the running of the college.

The girls who attended Vassar were trailblazers in many ways and Vassar graduates have gone on to become authors, politicians, scientists, and Academy Award winners. Vassar graduates include: Edna St. Vincent Millay, the first woman to win the Pulitzer Prize for Poetry; Helen C. Putnam, the first woman gynecologist; Bernadine Healy, the first woman to head the National Institute of Health; Vicki Miles-Lagrange, the first African-American woman to be sworn in as United States Attorney General; and Meryl Streep, the Academy Award winning actress. All students brought to the college a unique spirit. Spirited, passionate women tend to leave strong imprints behind in the places they lived and worked. This is very true of the Vassar campus.

You can find a statue of founder, Matthew Vassar, on the front lawn of the main building. Though long departed, Matthew Vassar is still seen all around the campus. He is said to haunt the fourth floor of the main building. People have reported seeing a man in late nineteenth century clothing walking the halls...and then *vanishing*. Matthew Vassar has also been seen walking the grounds and in other areas of the campus. Take a good look at his statue and then keep a good look out for him, usually at dusk and dawn.

Many of the spirits of the young women who attended Vassar never left — and they haunt all parts of the campus. The Main Hall, the oldest building on the campus, is said to be teeming with ghosts. Perhaps these halls remain haunted because it was the only college of its kind and the only place these young women felt intellectually accepted and, therefore, they want to remain where they felt happiest. In many cases, attending Vassar was the only chance these women had to pursue their academic and intellectual interests. Rooms 422 and 423 are said to be haunted by young women students of the nineteenth century. Sightings of young women in period dress are still reported, as are sounds of footsteps and doors opening and closing. Several girls were said to have committed suicide in the main hall and their ghosts still walk the hallways and rooms.

The ghost of Gertrude Angeline Bronson, class of 1895, is said to haunt room 318 of the main building. Many reports have been made of objects moving, temperature changes and the feeling of "being watched" have occurred in this room. According to legend, Gertrude was murdered and her murder was covered up. Many people have reported the figure of a woman, described as wearing Victorian clothes, standing by the window gazing sadly to the lawn below. She then slowly fades away.

Pratt House is haunted by a ghost who is only friendly to Vassar College students and staff. Pratt house is used to house guests of the college. The ghost will disturb those who are not affiliated with the college. The ghost will pester these visitors by tapping on shoulders, pulling hair and pulling off covers in the night. Guests have reported being shaken awake, hearing noises, and being touched.

I spoke with a relative of a woman who had worked at Vassar in the 1940s as a "house mother." According to this woman, there were constant noises, sounds of footsteps, and shuffling even when the girls had left for holidays. The "house mother" just thought the noises were "happy ghosts" of girls who used to live in the dorm and she largely ignored them.

Other areas of the campus that are haunted are the physics lab, the fifth floor of Davidson, and the Observatory. Girls have been seen as "vaporizing" through walls, making shuffling noises and opening doors.

Take a guided tour of the campus and snap pictures!

Visiting Vassar College

> † Vassar College, 124 Raymond Avenue, Poughkeepsie, New York 12604
> Phone: 845-437-7399
> Website: www.vassar.edu
> Email: admissions@vassar.edu

The website has all the information you need about visiting Vassar as well as a map to get around campus. Enter the grounds through the security gate. You will need a pass to visit. The best time to visit is on weekends or when classes are not in session.

~~~~~

Poughkeepsie Rural Cemetery

This cemetery is found just outside the city of Poughkeepsie. The cemetery was first established in 1852 overlooking the Hudson River. It is a very large cemetery encompassing two hundred acres of rolling, park-like landscape. I strongly recommend you stop at the gate and get a map before visiting or visit the cemetery's website for a copy of the map. Yes, I *did* get lost in this cemetery! I now just bring a map with me. It is the final resting place of several famous people among whom are; William and Andrew Smith, sons of the founder of the Smith Brothers Cough Drops; Matthew Vassar, founder of Vassar College; Honorable Smith Thompson, U.S. Supreme Court Justice from 1823-1843. General George Armstrong Custer was also buried here, but he was later interred in the Cemetery at West Point.

All of the ghost hunters I have spoken with are in agreement: this cemetery is *very* haunted. There are many spirits, which haunt the grounds. People have related stories of strange glowing orbs of light that can be seen floating after dark. Human voices can be heard as if whispering or mumbling. Dark, shadowy figures have been reported floating around and through gravestones.

Matthew Vassar's grave in the Poughkeepsie Rural Cemetery is in the shape of an acorn.

Visiting Poughkeepsie Rural Cemetery

† Poughkeepsie Rural Cemetery, 342 South Avenue, Poughkeepsie, New York 12602-0977.
   Phone: 845-454-6020
   Website: www.poughkeepsieruralcemetery.org

The Poughkeepsie Rural Cemetery offers an informative walking tour. You can find the tour and the map at their website or you may stop in the main office during business hours for a map.

Remember, never visit a cemetery after dark.

~~~~~

Christ Episcopal Church

Christ Episcopal Church in Poughkeepsie is a stone structure built in 1888, though the parish dates back to 1766. This church is known for its artistic stained glass windows. Like many churches, this one is haunted. The ghost of the former Rector, Dr. Alexander Griswold Cummings is reportedly still serving his parishioners now in ghostly form. He has been seen many times since his death in the early 1950s. As pastor, fearing fire, he did not like using candles. He often did not light them or blew them out the second services were over. After his death, candles used during services were repeatedly blown out. Reports of doors opening and closing and the sound of footsteps have all been attributed to the former pastor. Dr. Cummings seemed to quiet down after awhile only to be stirred back up when the rector's office was moved. Dr. Cummings office was converted to the church library and congregants claimed that the library was always freezing and attempts to warm it up were futile. It was this way for several years after the renovation but eventually, the spirit accepted this move and allowed the library to feel cozy and warm. But every once in awhile, people still report a cold chill or a light breeze in the library. It seems Dr. Cummings is still keeping an eye on his flock.

The church also has another ghost. An elderly woman parishioner, who died during services in the early 1900s, still haunts her familiar pew. Her spirit is seen halfway towards the back of the church. People claim to notice her, often when the church is empty, believing she is there to pray alone but if they turn away and then turn back she has disappeared. Some people, who sit in that area, claim to feel her presence or an odd ghostly chill.

Visiting Christ Episcopal Church

† Christ Episcopal Church, 20 Carroll Street, Poughkeepsie, New York 12601
  Phone: 845-452-8220
  Website: www.christchurchpok.org

The church is located at the corner of Academy and Barclay Streets in Poughkeepsie. Parking is available on the street.

Remember that Christ Episcopal Church is not a museum; it is a church used for private worship. You are welcome to join the congregants at worship. The church also hosts many events, which you are also welcome to attend.

~~~~~

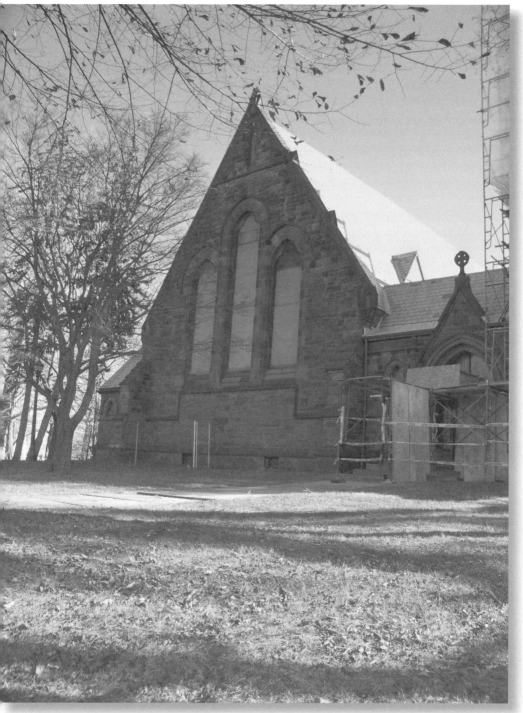

Christ Episcopal Church, Poughkeepsie... A former rector blows out candles, still in fear of fire.

Bardavon Opera House

When we think of ghosts, we think of scary apparitions. This is not the case in the Bardavon Theater in Poughkeepsie. The ghost of the Bardavon is highly regarded among the employees there. He is seen as a friend and protective spirit of the theater.

The Bardavon Opera House is the oldest continuously operating theater in New York State. Built in 1869, the Bardavon was originally called the Collingwood Opera House after its owner, James Collingwood. Collingwood, originally from England, had become one of Poughkeepsie's richest businessmen through his coal and lumber business. The Bardavon has hosted many a famous name throughout the years, including Sara Bernhardt, Mark Twain, Martha Graham, and Frank Sinatra.

Roger was a stage manager at the Bardavon in the late 1800s. He was killed accidentally on the stage when a stray bullet from a fight, which had broken out in the street just in front of the theater, pierced his heart. Soon after Roger's death, strange happenings began in the

The Bardavon Theater, Poughkeepsie... A protective spirit named Roger is credited with saving the Bardavon from being burned down.

theater, though nothing sinister. Doors seemed to open and close of their own volition. Lights that had been turned off at night were found to be on in the morning. Though Roger was a beloved ghost, employees found it unnerving to continually find things moved so they made a deal with Roger. The Bardavon has a "ghost light," which is turned on after everyone is done working for the day. When the ghost light is on, Roger knows that its ok to come out and he won't accidentally scare anyone who is there working.

Roger is credited with saving the Bardavon from being destroyed by fire. One day the employees arrived to find the theater filled with smoke. They searched everywhere for the source of the fire but to no avail. One employee, walking across the stage, happened to look up and there, impossibly, was a man in the rigging. He was pointed upwards towards the ceiling above the stage, which is several stories high. The employee immediately ran to the ladder affixed to the wall and climbed all the way up to the ceiling. There, in the ceiling space, the fire was raging. The arriving fire department was immediately directed to the source of the fire, enabling them to put the fire out quickly, thereby saving the Bardavon. Who was the man in the rigging? The employees have no doubt; it was Roger. When driving by the Bardavon, look for Roger's name on the Marquis.

The Bardavon also has a younger ghost. The theater was built directly in front of James Collingwood's coal business. While the theater was being built, a young girl, age 7 or 8, was killed by a coal truck on the property. There are reports of a girl in Victorian style dress in the balcony at night. She is dressed in pink and walks along the landing. Employees working on the stage often report looking up and seeing her in the balcony area.

Seeing a show in the Bardavon is a treat. But if you can't make a show, the Bardavon gives tours to the public for a nominal charge.

Visiting the Bardavon

† Bardavon, 35 Market Street, Poughkeepsie, New York 12601
Phone: 845-473-5288
Website: www.bardavon.org

Parking is sometimes difficult. I suggest parking in one of the parking garages near the theater. Do not park in areas that require a permit or are restricted. Your car will be "booted" and it will cost you a fine.

~~~~~

Dutchess County Community College

Bowne Hall

Bowne Hall is the oldest building on the grounds of Dutchess County Community College. This building was originally built in 1913 as the Nettie Bowne Hospital, an early tubercular sanatorium. It originally had three hospital buildings, but only Bowne Hall still stands. After treatments for tuberculosis improved, the hospital closed in 1956. The buildings and grounds were donated in 1957 and formed the campus of the Dutchess County Community College. At one time, the hospital building was the main academic building of the campus. It is now, after extensive renovation, the administration building.

The building has been restored, but still looks very much like those early tubercular sanatoriums. The long banks of windows running the length of the entire building were the open porches where tubercular patients received fresh air and sunshine as treatment for their illness. The basement of Bowne Hall was the hospital's morgue. Maintenance personnel have reported strange happenings such as a "weird" presence,

Bowne Hall, Dutchess County Community College, Poughkeepsie. Spirits of nurses and patients still wander this old hospital.

strange unaccountable footsteps, and the elevator moving from floor to floor uncalled and odd noises. People report hearing footsteps in the hall and there has even been a report of the strange scent of urine on one of the upper floors. Some of these disturbances have caused some maintenance staff to be wary of entering the basement alone.

As part of my paranormal research, I was invited, with my fellow investigators, on an investigative tour of Bowne Hall. The building is quite large and, for security purposes, we were only given access to public areas, such as hallways, lobbies, bathroom areas, and of course, the morgue area. As usual, the "techies" went to work setting up the recording devices and other electronic devices to capture evidence. The morgue area, originally been one large room, was now divided into two smaller rooms. There was a small hallway and another room, farther down the hall, packed with file cabinets. Noises started almost immediately as we were setting up. We were aware that basements are loaded with pipes that make all sorts of noises so we tried not to jump to conclusions. However, an investigator, who did not believe in "ghosts," came out of the file storage room in a bit of a hurry. He claimed he heard an "animal noise" and was afraid that a raccoon had gotten into the storage room. We all went in, put the lights on and searched the room meticulously. We found no animals or animal droppings. We turned the light off and the investigator went back in to set up his EVP equipment. He again came out and claimed he heard the "animal noise" again. Several investigators, myself included, joined him. We all heard growling, which did indeed sound like an animal. We again searched the room and could find no source of the growling.

In the morgue area, several of our investigators could hear the sound of a human voice though the words were indistinguishable. We doubled checked with our host (who, by the way, waited outside) and he assured us that no one was in the building except the investigators and we were "locked in." All the while we were investigating, the elevator moved, by itself, from floor to floor, the door opening, as if waiting for an unseen passenger and then taking off to another floor.

All of the investigators saw a dark shadowy figure in the morgue area and many of us were able to catch this shadow on film. Many of the investigators experienced heaviness in their chest, shortness of breath and the feeling of being cold.

Our investigation of the upper floors revealed less sinister feelings. On the third floor, we all experienced an office light turning on and then several minutes later we noticed the light was off. We carefully checked the office door, but it was locked. We contacted our host and he again, assured us, that no one else was in the building. As we were investigating the light, a toilet flushed behind us in the women's room. Since we always investigate in pairs, we knew that no one of our investigative group could be in that bathroom. We entered the bathroom, the light was off, and controlled by an automatic sensor. The bathroom was empty. Since, we had a licensed plumber in the group, he investigated the toilet and found it in perfect working order and no reason to flush on its own. Several people in our group reported strange odors on the third floor; the passing scent of women's perfume and the smell of urine near the elevators.

The two mediums in the group, myself and another man, were able to sense the presence of many ghosts. It seems former patients and nurses are still roaming the hall tending to the business of healing the sick.

Visiting Bowne Hall

† Dutchess County Community College, 53 Pendell Road, Poughkeepsie, New York 12601-1595
  Phone: 845-431-8000
  Website: www.sunydutchess.edu

There is a large student lot across the road from the main campus. You will have to climb up a moderate climb but there are stairs and a ramp with railings. You can visit Bowne Hall during regular office hours. The lobby area includes historic pictures of the sanatorium. Keep your ears and your nose open! Remember this is a place of business and you cannot just "wander around." However, you are welcome to visit the lobby area, look at the historic display and take pictures.

~~~~~

Marist College

Marist College was founded in 1929 along the banks of the Hudson River. It was originally a seminary to educate Catholic men in preparation for the Marist Brotherhood. It is now one of the top colleges in the country with a student body of over 5,000 co-eds. As you walk on campus, you can see sweeping vistas of the Hudson River. Like many college campuses, Marist has its resident ghosts.

In 1974, Shelley Sperling was a freshman at Marist College. She was intelligent, talented and beautiful. Tragedy struck in February 1975 when a jealous ex-boyfriend followed her to campus and shot her dead in the campus cafeteria. Ever since, there have been reported sightings of Shelley in Sheahan Hall, her freshman residence, and the cafeteria. Christina Hope, a former student and resident assistant of Sheahan Hall, told me she experienced an apparition of Shelley personally.

Sheehan Hall, Marist College, Poughkeepsie... Shelley Sperling, who was senselessly murdered, is still said to walk the halls of her old dormitory.

"One day I was working on the website and I had photocopies of her yearbook picture and her boyfriend's lying on my bed. (This was when I was an RA in Sheahan.) I had left my dorm room door propped open with a laundry detergent bottle and went to do "a round." When I came back, I saw a girl with long brown hair and a crocheted sweater of cream, white, brown and tan looking at the pictures. When I walked in, she looked up at me, and then disappeared into the wall. I opened the closet door and the bathroom door and did not see her."

Christina was convinced the girl she saw in her room was Shelley and maintains a website in her honor.

Other people on campus also claim to have seen her. Most of the ghostly activity takes place right in Sheahan Hall. People report doors opening and closing, sounds of footsteps and, strange but true, coming into the laundry to find their clothes neatly folded and stacked when no one else had been in the laundry room.

While the dormitory is off limits to visitors, you can visit the memorial on campus. People claim to have seen Shelley there as well. But students claim that Shelley is not the only Marist student walking around campus. There have been reports of other spirits wandering campus.

Visiting Marist College

† Marist College, 3399 North Road, Poughkeepsie, New York 12601
Phone: 845.575.3000
Website: www.christinahope.com/shelley_project/what/what.html or www.marist.edu

Due to limitations in parking, it is best to visit the Marist campus on the weekends or when school is not in session. Marist hosts many sporting events, which attract very large crowds. Parking is almost impossible at these times. Therefore, check the Marist sports schedules online before visiting. The website is maintained by Christina Hope in honor of Shelley Sperling.

~~~~~

Mid-Hudson Psychiatric Center

The Mid-Hudson Psychiatric Center is now closed. It was originally named the Hudson River State Hospital. The center was opened in 1869. At its height of operation, the hospital housed 9,000 patients. It has a large campus-like design. It was designed by Calvert Vaux, who also designed the grounds of Wilderstein, the Point, and Central Park in Manhattan. The main building at the hospital is designated as a National Historic Landmark. When it was built, psychiatric hospitals were designed for people to stay for long periods of time, as opposed to today, where the focus is on healing and returning people to their lives. Some people spent years at psychiatric hospitals, others more spent most of their adult lives there. As you can imagine, most of the older psychiatric hospitals are filled with troubled spirits. Many hospitals are haunted, particularly those that deal with the most difficult cases. People came to these hospitals under great stress, many times against their will, and their energy lingers. People have reported hearing loud noises after dark. People have also reported hearing troubled screams. Footsteps can be heard echoing in the halls, doors open and close for no reason. People claim they have seen "shadowy figure" wandering the grounds. Psychiatric hospitals tend to attract shadow people. Many people have reported a deep sense of feeling "ill-at-ease" even just passing the grounds. I spoke with a man who was allowed access to the hospital for an investigation and he said it was one of the scariest and disturbing places he had ever visited. Not only did he hear unexplained noises, he saw dark shadowy figures lurking at the end of hallways and felt a sense of terror the entire time he investigated the hall and rooms.

While the grounds are closed to visitors, you can still drive by this site. I am hoping that soon this site will be converted into something usable so it is open to the public. It is located on Route 9 in Poughkeepsie opposite Marist College. You can see some of the grounds from the road.

Chapter Ten:
Hyde Park

Culinary Institute of America

Even if it wasn't haunted, the Culinary Institute of America (CIA) is a place you just can't miss visiting in the Hudson Valley. What makes the visit just that much more delightful is the spirits of gentle Jesuit brothers haunting the halls.

The campus of the Culinary Institute offers breathtaking views of the Hudson River. You can lounge on the Culinary Institute's 30,000 square foot Roman style terrace over looking the Hudson. The campus operates five award-winning restaurants: St. Andres Café, Ristorante Catherine de' Medici, the Escoffier, American Bounty Restaurant, and the Apple Pie

Roth Hall, Culinary Institute of American, Hyde Park... Jesuit brothers still wander the halls in prayer.

Bakery. Each restaurant, staffed by students, is open to the public. Dining at the CIA is a treat you will not forget. Ghost hunting has never been more delicious. Tours are available, and the campus also has a wonderful gift shop.

But before CIA opened in 1972, the campus was the St. Andrew-on-the-Hudson Jesuit Seminary. Thomas Fortune Ryan was a benefactor of the Jesuits and, as was often the custom, to honor the Ryan family, when a member of the family died, he or she was buried under the altar at chapel of St. Andrew. The chapel is located in the center of campus and can be accessed through the Roth building. The CIA has converted St. Andrew's Chapel into its dining hall, with little renovation. It still contains the hand painted frescos on the walls and ceilings. However, the Ryans had to be moved. They were dug up and re-interred in the cemetery on the campus. The Jesuits still maintain the cemetery.

As most ghost hunters know, disturbing the peace of those laid to rest often creates restless spirits...and this seems to be the case at the CIA. Roth Hall, one of the original halls, and the old chapel area are haunted. Doors open and close by themselves. Employees working late report heavy footsteps on the main staircase in Roth Hall. Witnesses have also reported seeing Jesuit ghosts floating placidly about in their very distinctive robes and passing through doors and walls.

The cemetery at Culinary Institute of America... Ghostly orbs have been seen in the cemetery.

Grave of Pierre Teilhard de Chardin... The Jesuit brother, paleontologist, biologist, philosopher, and author reposes here.

Another haunted area of the campus is the cemetery. The cemetery is set back from the main campus and is locked. You can get permission to visit the cemetery at the security office. Jesuits priests, novitiates and members of the Ryan family are all buried in these simple graves. Any new burials, after the CIA took over the grounds, are in the Ryan Mausoleum at the back of the cemetery. Pierre Teilhard de Chardin is buried in this graveyard. A Jesuit, paleontologist, and philosopher, Teilhard de Chardin is best known for his book *The Phenomenon of Man.* Though all the gravestones are exactly the same, you will have little difficulty finding Teilhard de Chardin's, as it receives many visitors who leave behind mementos. Gentle spirits who can be seen walking in pensive thought at dusk, their feet just slightly off the ground, are said to haunt this cemetery.

Visiting the Culinary Institute of America

† The Culinary Institute of America, Route 9, Hyde Park, New York
Phone: 800-285-4627
Website: www.ciachef.edu

Since this is such a delightful place to visit, I suggest you start your visit with a guided tour. Park in the parking garage in front of Roth Hall and stop by the hospitality desk, just inside the front doors. If you plan to eat at the Culinary other than at the Apple Pie Bakery Cafe, you must make reservations. Remember, students run the restaurants so they are only open when school is in session. For reservations, call 845-471-6608.

A photo ID is required to visit the cemetery. Keys for the cemetery can be obtained in the security office.

~~~~~

Springwood

In Hyde Park, right off Route 9, is Springwood, the birthplace and home of Franklin D. Roosevelt, the thirty-second president of the United States. Also located at the Springwood site is the first Presidential Library, designed by FDR himself in Dutch Colonial style. There is a museum, which holds an extensive display of the personal items of FDR and his wife, Eleanor.

The Roosevelts' lives were full of greatness of all kinds: great courage, great leadership, great happiness, and ... great sadness. All of these feelings pervade the grounds of Springwood, from the house to the stable and even to the rose garden where Franklin, Eleanor, and their beloved dog, Fala, are buried.

Springwood is a place haunted by "impressions." Impressions are what people leave behind when a place is associated with great emotion. Springwood holds these emotions within its walls and grounds.

Springwood is a plaster colored Greek Revival style mansion. Originally, a large farmhouse, the Roosevelts' expanded and updated the home to fit

Springwood, Hyde Park... The home of President Franklin D. Roosevelt. Franklin's mother, Sara Roosevelt, is said to still be receiving guests.

Old Home Road, Springwood... President Roosevelt can be seen walking, using crutches, up and down this road.

their growing family and status. Approaching it, the house gives a sense of grandeur but not haughtiness. It is decorated with almost incongruent sea foam green shutters.

Before entering the house, take a look down the long straight drive. The original driveway to the house, the family called this drive "Old Home Road." It is on this drive that Franklin rehabilitated himself after his affliction with polio. Using crutches, he went up and down this long drive to strengthen his arms and upper body. There have been several claims by guests to the estate, often out of the peripheral vision, of a figure on this road. He is best seen at dusk, just before the grounds close. See if you can catch a glimpse of this figure. Is it Franklin on crutches exercising his arms?

As you enter the house through the small white portico and double doors, the smell of "oldness" will assault your senses. All of the contents of the home, except the carpeting, are original to the time when Franklin, Eleanor and the children lived there. Sensitives have reported the feeling of children in the house. However, the spirit most seen and felt is Sara Delano Roosevelt, Franklin's mother.

Franklin's father, James, was married twice. His first wife, Rebecca, died in 1876, leaving one grown son. Sara was James' second wife. James was 52 and Sara was 26 when they married. They had one son, Franklin, whom both parents adored. Franklin's father died in 1900. Franklin was 18 and had just started his freshman year at Harvard. Sara became the family matriarch living at Springwood. Franklin brought his wife, Eleanor, and their children to live with his mother. Eleanor found Sara overbearing. Eleanor's life was not happy at Springwood. Perhaps, it is Eleanor's spirit of sadness that you can feel in several areas of the house.

It is Sara's presence that still pervades the house today. Sara has been seen in her sitting room on the first floor and in the dining room, still presiding over social functions of the family. If you hear the rustle of skirts, it's most likely Sara on the steps coming to receive guests.

Many people leaving the estate claim to have felt a great sense of sadness. This would most likely be Eleanor. Franklin and Eleanor, though a professional couple, were not happily married. Sara had opposed Franklin's marriage to Eleanor and did everything to stop it. Later in the marriage, Eleanor found out about Franklin's affair with Eleanor's social secretary, Lucy Mercer. In 1918, Eleanor found love letters written from Lucy to Franklin. A devastated Eleanor considered a divorce but Sara would not hear of it. She threatened to disinherit Franklin if he divorced. Franklin promised to never see Lucy alone again. However, their marriage never fully recovered. When marriages decline, many couples occupy separate bedrooms. The Roosevelts got separate houses. Franklin remained at Springwood and Eleanor eventually would reside at Val-Kill, a near by property. Though politely called Eleanor's "retreat" it was really, where she could get away from her overbearing mother-in-law and her husband. While visiting Springwood, particularly in family areas and Eleanor's small bedroom, you can feel a sense of sadness.

Outside, in the rose garden, where the graves of Eleanor and Franklin reside, a figure of a man has been seen. Many people assume he is a visitor but notice when they turn away and then turn back he has vanished. While no one has yet identified him, perhaps its Franklin visiting the home he loved.

Also, in front of Springwood, is an old "mile post marker" on Route 9. I have had several reports of a man "leaning" on this mile marker. What's odd is that he can only be seen when you look backwards through your rearview mirror. So, if you are leaving Springwood and headed south, keep checking your rearview mirror. Maybe you will spot this man; perhaps it is Franklin resting at the end of Old Home Road.

Visiting Springwood

† National Park Service, 4097 Albany Post Road (Route 9), Hyde Park, New York 12538
    Phone: 800-FDR-VISIT
    Website: www.nps.gov/hofr

Springwood is open year-round except for Thanksgiving, Christmas, and New Year's Day from 9 a.m. to 5 p.m. Admission to the grounds and burial site is free. There is a fee to tour the house and museum.

Chapter Eleven:

Staatsburg

The Point
(Hoyt Mansion)

If you are going to visit this haunted mansion, you will have to hike, as there is no longer any direct access to the house. Though there are dire stories of murder and suicide surrounding the mansion, the real reason for this abandoned gem is really rather mundane.

The Point, also sometimes referred to as the Hoyt Mansion after the family who built it, was constructed in 1855. This Gothic Revival home was designed by famous architect, Calvert Vaux, who co-designed Central

The Point, Staatsburg... Sounds from a former resident can still be heard.

Park, the Mid-Hudson Psychiatric Center, and the grounds of Wilderstein. The Point is designated a National Historic Landmark. The house once had views of the Hudson, but now the property has suffered from almost a half century of abandonment and neglect.

How does a jewel of the Hudson become an abandoned house? The story goes that Mr. Hoyt killed himself and his whole family. Unfortunately, this story is entirely fabricated. Most likely, the story was made up by some campers looking to scare their friends around a campfire at Norrie State Park. The real story is more mundane. In 1934, the sister of Margaret Lewis Norrie donated her estate to New York State to create the Lewis Norrie State Park. In 1938, the Mills Estate was donated to New York by Margaret Phipps, the daughter of Ogden and Ruth Livingston Mills, the last residents of the house. The Hoyt property cut a forty-acre swath between these two now state-owned properties. In the 1960s, New York wanted to purchase the Hoyt Mansion and make the three properties one large state park. When the Hoyt's refused to sell, the state took the mansion through the process of Eminent Domain. The plan had been to raze the mansion and put in a swimming pool complex. Thankfully, the money for the pool never materialized and the mansion was left standing, though not maintained. Most literature about the park doesn't even mention the Hoyt's or their estate.

The house has suffered from years of vandalism and lack of maintenance. At this time, efforts to restore Hoyt's Mansion are well underway. Currently, you may visit the house, but you may not enter it. I'm hoping that sometime in the not to distance future, the mansion will be open to the public. However, you can still get close enough to get some great pictures.

The house and surrounding area are said to be haunted. People have reported the sound of indistinct human voices, sounds from inside the mansion, such as footsteps or things being moved about, even though the mansion is empty. You will love the haunted feel of this place. Take plenty of pictures.

The Calvert Vaux Preservation Alliance is in the process of restoring this historic home. You may find more information about the house and the restoration at www.calvertaux.org.

Visiting the Point

† From the Mills Mansion, Staatsburg, NY:

You may park at Mills Mansion and hike along the river to the Mansion. Parking is free. Traveling on Route 9 either north or south, turn onto Old Post Road to Staatsburg. The main entrance is on Old Post Road.

Once you have parked, walk directly down to the Hudson River. Stay on the trail with the white trail marker. The Point will be on your left. Keep looking up. You'll see its roof and you can hike up the embankment.

† Contact information for Mills Mansion:

Staatsburg State Historic Site, P.O. Box 308, Staatsburg, NY 12580; 845-889-8851

~~~

† From Norrie State Park:

The entrance to Norrie State Park is also in Staatsburg on Old Post Road. Park in any parking lot and look for a map to find the white trail marker. It's not too hard; head to the river and turn right. The Point will be on your right.

† Contact information for Norrie State Park:

Norrie State Park, Old Post Road, P.O. Box 893, Staatsburg, New York 12580; 845-889-4646

While this is a scenic hike in some parts, it's also very narrow with drop-offs to the Hudson River below. Wear good hiking shoes and watch for poison ivy.

Parks close at dusk. Give yourself adequate time to hike back before it becomes dark. Camping is available in the park from mid-May through October.

Chapter Twelve:

Millbrook

Bennett College

Halcyon Hall

The main building of Bennett College started out as a hotel. H. J. Davidson, Jr built Halcyon Hall in 1893; it is a rambling building reminiscent of the Gilded Age in American history. The building, located at Routes 343 and 44, now stands in ruins. It was used as a hotel for eight years and then after that time it stood vacant until 1907 when Miss May F. Bennett purchased the building for a girls' school. The school was originally founded in Irvington, New York, and after renovation of the hotel, moved to Millbrook. The school transformed itself from a finishing school for girls into a two-year college and finally a four-year college. It closed it doors in 1978. It has stood unoccupied since its closing. Time has since ravaged the campus.

Bennett College, Millbrook. Orbs of lights and sounds of footsteps have been heard in this now abandoned building.

Bennett College, Millbrook. Noises attributed to past students can still be heard in this building.

Vandals have broken into the ruins, and, like many places, left adolescent attempts at "devil" worship. Signs of pentagrams and fires can be seen in old pictures. What most young people who do this sort of thing don't realize is that it can actually attract spiritual activity. The spirits attracted to this type of activity are often opportunistic spirits; that is, spirits that are looking for an outlet or a portal. They may have been people who were disturbed in their incarnate life or disincarnate spirits who are looking for a place to "attach." Some people refer to these types of spirits as "vampire" spirits because they are looking for energy to channel.

At Bennett College, there are two types of hauntings: the residual imprints of the students who attended Bennett and the opportunistic spirits attracted by trespassers seeking paranormal experiences. Like many places that experienced happy times, the Bennett College is haunted by the energy of all the people who lived and worked there. Before the building became inaccessible, there were many reports of footsteps, door closings and unexplained noises. At this time, the Halcyon Hall may still be standing but there are plans to demolish it. A demolition will not remove the spiritual energy at this place. The new condominiums being built on these beautiful grounds may experience some residual hauntings.

If Halcyon Hall is still standing, keep in mind that you may not enter it. It is extremely dangerous. I am hopeful, however, that in the future the area will be open for people to visit. For now, park on the road (there is a pull-off spot) and take pictures. You may be able to catch a ghost in one of your pictures. Since the place looks haunted, it's a good spot to have lunch in the car and tell scary stories to each other.

Chapter Thirteen:

Dover Plains

Old Drovers Inn

A great haunted place to stay while visiting the Hudson Valley is the Old Drovers Inn. If you don't want to stay the night, you can dine where the drovers dined. First opened in 1750 by John Preston, the Inn gets it name from the "cattle drovers" who used to stop there before the Revolutionary War while driving cattle from New England to New York. According to reports, the inn has been haunted since its earliest days. One ghost is said to be that of a Tory doctor who hanged himself rather than serve in the newly forming Continental Army. He is a loud and boisterous spirit slamming doors, pacing hallways and rattling door handles. He will turn on lights in empty rooms. I suppose he is still angry about the colonies winning the war.

The Inn is known today for its delicious gourmet food and fine antique décor. There are also tastefully decorated, upscale rooms available for the night. There are only seven guest rooms so reservations must be made in advance. Don't worry, though, my sources tell me the ghosts never bothers overnight guests.

Visiting Old Drovers Inn

† Old Drovers Inn, 196 East Duncan Hill Road, Dover Plains, New York 12522

Phone: 845-832-9311

Website: www.olddroversinn.com

Email: info@olddroversinn.com

Chapter Fourteen

Wassaic

Village of Wassaic

The name Wassaic is derived from a Native American word meaning "Narrow River." Some also say that the word means "land of difficult access" and a trip to the hamlet will explain why. This village is nestled in a little crook or hollow, easily bypassed if you don't know where to turn. Now it looks like a struggling community, but, at one time, this little village was a gem.

Noah Gridley established an iron foundry in Wassaic in 1825. His furnace was tremendously successful and he became a rich man. Assisting in his success was his friend, Cornelius Vanderbilt. Being an astute businessman, Gridley convinced Vanderbilt to build the railroad through Wassaic so it would be easier for Gridley to move his iron. Noah Gridley also convinced another friend, Gail Borden, to build his new innovative condensed milk factory in Wassaic. Borden supplied the Union troops with condensed milk during the Civil War and he became a wealthy man himself.

Noah Gridley is said to have really loved Wassaic and the surrounding area; he built a house in town. After Gridley's death, his house was sold to another family. However, it appears that old Noah still inhabits his former residence. The current owner claims that every night at the same time her cat will wake suddenly and, appearing startled, look to the stairs and then go down the stairs into the kitchen. It appears that Noah Gridley's bedtime ritual was to go downstairs for a glass of milk. Noah now has a buddy with him at milk time.

Other homes are also said to be haunted in this old community and there's also a kind of "imprint" haunting from the Revolutionary War days. General George Washington and his troops passed through Wassaic on their way to Connecticut during the Revolutionary War. People still claim to see the spirits of the soldiers in Revolutionary garb, tired and disheveled, near the stream.

Many of the old homes in Wassaic sport their own ghosts including the Benham House on Mygatt Road; Mygatt was named after the family who originally owned the house, which, though remodeled through the centuries, was built in the 1700s. It went through a cycle of rebuilding and eventual decline before finally being refurbished to its former glory. During its renovation, the workmen would often remark how their tools had moved during the night. The owners were a bit concerned, afraid someone was breaking in during the night, however, nothing was ever reported missing; it was just moved. When the house was finished, the owners rented it out. The tenants have all reported seeing a young man leaving the barn. Over the years, the different tenants have run out to see who was trespassing and never found anyone. They all describe the young man the same and he appears to be the same spirit many of them see. Some of the tenants have also reported seeing a woman in a long skirt leaving one of the parlors and several of the them have reported waking and seeing a man standing at the end of their beds.

Finally, just north of Wassaic is the Wassaic Developmental Center. It was established in 1930 as a training school for the mentally disabled. At one time, it housed up to 3,500 people. While no one shared their stories specific about the center, I have no doubts that it is haunted. Just drive around and tell me what you think. I did talk with a person who interviewed for a job there when it was opened and he said the "energy" there was so disturbing that, when offered the job, he did not take it.

Visiting Wassaic

† Wassaic is located on old State Route 22, Wassaic. Do not miss the turn off from the new Route 22. There is a small public parking area and walk past the old furnace and factory.

† Wassaic Developmental Center is located on County Route 81, Wassaic, New York 12592

Chapter Fifteen:

Clinton

Fiddler's Bridge

There is a narrow, winding country road in Clinton called Fiddler's Bridge Road. In the early 1800s, the road was sparsely populated with only a farm here and there. In those days, men with musical talent often made a little extra money by playing for local parties. A good musician, usually a fiddler, could make a tidy sum of money playing for weddings and parties. On September 7, 1808, a local man, known for his fiddling ability, was on his way home after playing most of the night and well into the morning. It was late and very dark. He probably still had the fiddling tunes playing in his head and images of the town's maids dancing happily to his fiddle music. Upon reaching a small bridge, he was assaulted and subsequently murdered. Did he know his assailant? No one knows. There seems to have been no reason for such a brutal attack. In the morning, his body and smashed fiddle were found under the bridge. Murder was relatively uncommon in this area, particularly to poor, unarmed fiddlers. Word spread rapidly of the fiddler's murder. No one was ever caught and his murder remains a mystery. The road and bridge were later named Fiddler's Bridge. According to tradition, the Fiddler can be heard playing his fiddle nightly between 10 p.m. and midnight.

Fiddler's Bridge, Clinton.... The unsolved murder of an unarmed fiddler took place here.

It would be an interesting story even if it just ended there. However, to "celebrate" the 100th anniversary of the Fiddler's murder, the town supervisor led an excursion out to the bridge of some interested town folk. Of course, they timed their excursion to arrive at the bridge at midnight. An article in the September 10, 1908 edition of the *Poughkeepsie Daily Eagle* claims all members of the excursion heard the fiddler playing. People claim to have seen the fiddler near the bridge, as well.

Neighbors report feeling "eerie" when they are near the bridge. The town historian still conducts excursions out to the bridge — the site of the town's most famous murder. Though you can no longer cross over the original bridge, the site of the murder is easy to locate because the town erected a sign on the site. Be very careful if you are going to visit the site, as it is located on a sharp turn. It is best to park where you can pull your car all the way off the road. Wear bright colored clothes and carry a flashlight if you are visiting at night. Listen for cars...and fiddle music.

Visiting Fiddler's Bridge

† From 9G turn onto Hollow Road and then make a left onto Fiddler's Bridge Road; the sign will be on your left.

† From Clinton, follow Fiddler's Bridge Road. The sign will be on your right.

Chapter Sixteen:

Rhinebeck

Olde Rhinebeck Inn

If you're looking for a pleasantly haunted place to stay while in the Hudson Valley, you might want to choose the Olde Rhinebeck Inn. This is a restored inn built in the 1740s. As the family and its prosperity grew, the house was added onto, giving it a unique nature. The house, which belonged to a single family for over 239 years, is now a small bed and breakfast. The inn is lovingly haunted by a spirit named George — and "he" is known to walk the floors, open doors, and leave a trail of cigar smoke in his wake. One particular closet door in one of the guest's rooms will not stay closed — even when latched securely. George is blamed for this phenomenon. George is a friendly spirit that warmly welcomes the visitors

The Inn only has four guest rooms, so make your reservations well in advance of your anticipated visit.

Visiting the Olde Rhinebeck Inn

† Old Rhinebeck Inn, 340 Wurtemburg Road, Rhinebeck, New York 12572

Phone: 845-871-1745

Website: http://www.rhinebeckinn.com

~~~~~

Wilderstein

If you want to visit a place that *looks* haunted, Wilderstein is the place to go! Though it is a Queen Anne style mansion, its colors, described as chocolate brown and deep forest green, give it a creepy Gothic look. Wilderstein was the home of the Suckley (pronounced SOOK-ley) family and was built in 1852 by the patriarch, Thomas Suckley. The original home was an Italianate villa designed by John Warren Ritch. In 1888, Robert Suckley, Thomas's son, doubled the size of the house, adding a porch and a five-story tower. *(Every good haunted house has a tower!)* For this massive renovation, Suckley hired Arnout Cannon from Poughkeepsie as the architect and Joseph Burr Tiffany as the interior designer. *(Yes, you can expect to see those gorgeous Tiffany windows!)* Calvert Vaux designed the grounds.

The last of the Suckleys—and most famous—to live in the house was Margaret "Daisy" Suckley, the confidante and companion of Franklin Delano Roosevelt, as well as, rumored, his mistress. Letters found in an old, battered black suitcase under Daisy's bed after her death attest to her close, intimate relationship with the late president. However, the letters do not go as far as to admitting to a sexual relationship. Daisy gave the president his beloved dog, Fala, and was instrumental in the creation of the FDR Library in Hyde Park. She traveled extensively with FDR and was with him when he died in Warm Springs, Georgia.

As the family fortune dwindled, Daisy stubbornly remained in the mansion. She died in 1991, just short of her 100th birthday. By that time, the mansion had fallen into a decrepit state, appearing almost abandoned. In the end, Daisy was living in only two rooms of this huge mansion. She inhabited the library, which she used as a bedroom, and the butler's

Wilderstein, Rhinebeck... Daisy Suckley is still in residence and keeping an eye on renovations.

Daisy Suckley's bedroom exactly as she left it. A suitcase containing letters from Franklin D. Roosevelt, revealing an intimate friendship, was found under her bed. An orb appears over Daisy's bed.

pantry, which she had converted into a small kitchen. While watching a video of Daisy at Wilderstein, it is easy to understand that even though Daisy was physically living in a shell of her former life, in her mind, she was still living in grandeur. Where others saw a decaying mansion, she saw it just as it looked when it was newly painted in 1910. On the other hand, perhaps, she was able to see beyond the present into the future. Either way, because of Daisy's vision, this extraordinary example of an age long past is still available for all of us to gaze back...and see more than ghosts.

Daisy claimed the house to be haunted while she was still living there. According to Daisy, the ghost, an ethereal female spirit in Victorian costume, stayed in her part of the house while Daisy stayed in hers, so the two rarely crossed paths.

Many say that the ghost of Daisy lingers behind to oversee renovations. Employees report the pleasant scent of perfume in the second-story hallway. Even die-hard non-believers often claim to get a whiff of perfume when walking on the second-story landing. I was able to smell the perfume on a visit to the house. Is this the ghost of Daisy herself? Daisy, in the last interview before she died, claimed, "I can't imagine living anywhere else." I believe she is still there.

Before the house was opened to the public, a woman who was involved in the preservation efforts stayed overnight in one of the bedrooms. She awoke to footsteps and the sound of locks being clicked. She got up to check, but found no one in the house. The next day, when mentioning the strange event, she was told that it had probably been Robert, Daisy's long dead brother. In life, Robert had taken on the job of securing all the doors and windows prior to bedtime. Other people have claimed to hear Robert as well, walking about and "checking up on things."

Another person who has dedicated many hours to the preservation of Wilderstein also told me, "The spirits are here because they want to be."

I strongly urge you to visit Wilderstein. It is one of the most delightfully haunted places I have ever visited. Don't be surprised to catch a glimpse of Daisy having tea on the porch or a whiff of her perfume.

Visiting Wilderstein

† Wilderstein Historic Site, 330 Morton Road, Rhinebeck, New York

Phone: 845-876-4818
Website: www.wilderstein.org
Email: Wilderstein@wilderstein.org

~~~~~

Rhinecliff Hotel

The Rhinecliff is a tastefully restored and renovated 1854 hotel overlooking the Hudson River. It was designed by George Veitch, a well-known local architect who also designed the Rhinebeck Episcopal Church of the Messiah, St. Joseph's Roman Catholic Church, and District No. 2 School House.

The hotel was originally designed to serve travelers of the newly opened Hudson River Railroad and the Kingston-Rhinecliff Ferry. In its heyday, the hotel served as the center of Rhinecliff's business district and was in continuous operation from its opening in 1854 until it closed in 2003. By that time, it was in a serious state of decline. Two brothers, James and David Chapman were able to see its original beauty; they bought the hotel and meticulously restored it.

During the restoration, several pictures were taken by renovators of an ethereal mist. Employees of the hotel also report doors opening and closing on their own, as well as lights turning on and off. Most of the employees believe the ghost to be George Veitch, pleased with the way the hotel has been restored.

The Rhinecliff Hotel, Rhinecliff... George Veitch, the building's architect, is still overseeing renovations.

Visiting Rhinecliff Hotel

† The Rhinecliff, 4 Grinnel Street, Rhinecliff, New York 12574
Phone: 845-876-0590
Website: www.therhinecliff.com
Email: info@therhinecliff.com

You don't have to stay overnight to enjoy the hotel. The hotel, which boasts of its original bar, serves gourmet lunches and dinners. Since business tends to be seasonal, call for information or to make reservations. Since the Metro-North train station is directly in front of the hotel, you don't even need to take your car. However, if you do, the hotel has plenty of parking.

Chapter Seventeen:

Annandale-on-Hudson

Bard College

Blithewood Mansion

Blithewood is one of Hudson Valley's best-kept secrets. This gorgeous mansion, reminiscent of English manor houses, lies on expansive lawns with a formal, expertly maintained Italian walled garden. From the lawn, there are beautiful vistas of the Hudson River.

Colonel Peter Schuyler originally purchased the land in 1680 from the Native Americans. In the 1830s, Robert Donaldson purchased the property. It was Donaldson who named this idyllic setting Blithewood. He hired Andrew Jackson Downing to design the lawn. In 1899, Andrew Zabriskie, a dealer in antiquities and coins, purchased it and he hired Francis Hoppin to design the palatial estate. Zabriskie's family donated the estate to Bard College in 1951; it is now owned by the Levy Institute of Economics.

Blithewood, Bard College... The ghost of a young girl inhabits the lawn and garden.

The mansion is home to at least two spirits. One spirit is a poltergeist type ghost said to make noises, open and shut doors, and move items about. Another ghost is of a young girl, about 9-years-old, in Victorian style dress. She has been seen walking in the house and outside on the lawn.

Visiting Blithewood

† Blithewood, Bard College, Annandale-on-Hudson, New York
Phone: 845-758-7700
Website: www.levy.org
Email: info@levy.org

Unfortunately, Blithewood is not open to the public, though you may tour the grounds during daylight hours. I recommend visiting when college is not in session as it is easier to find parking. The garden is worth the visit alone and, since the spirit of the girl has been seen outside, you may be able to get a glimpse of her here. Visit in the summer when the garden is in full bloom.

Chapter Eighteen:

Germantown

Clermont

Pirates? On the Hudson? All well-haunted waterways have a pirate or two—and the Hudson is no exception.

The very wealthy Livingston family originally owned Clermont Mansion and the land surrounding it. The Livingstons were one of the richest and politically influential families during the formation of New York State and the United States, and they held many positions of power in local, state, and federal politics. Philip Livingston was a signer of the Declaration of Independence. The family in the Hudson River Valley goes back to 1673.

Clermont... The ghost of Captain Kidd still peers among the locust trees in search of his lost treasure.

Robert Livingston, the family's patriarch, was a good friend of Captain Kidd, the notorious pirate who is said to have left a treasure buried somewhere on the East Coast. Robert Livingston invested heavily in Kidd's "enterprises." Livingston, being a shrewd businessman, presented Captain Kidd with a "business deal": Livingston, along with several very other wealthy businessmen, would finance Captain Kidd, who would make his living by capturing pirates and their goods. Kidd was only to capture and loot pirate ships, thus only "privateering" rather than pirating, which of course, was illegal. He would then share his booty with his "investors." The stories of Kidd's success have mixed reviews. History says he was very unsuccessful and had very little to leave behind by the time of his execution for the crime of piracy on May 23, 1701. Other say Kidd was a shrewd businessman and pirate and spirited away most of his wealth and treasure.

Not only business partners, Livingston and Kidd were reportedly close friends as well. Kidd visited the Livingston's as a guest in their home on the Hudson and was reportedly fond of the Livingston children. Some say on the Livingston property is where Kidd's treasure was spirited away and safely buried.

The ghost of Captain Kidd has been seen on the property of Clermont. He is most often seen outside the house, standing among the locust trees looking out towards the Hudson. Is that where he buried his treasure? Many people believe that Livingston may have gotten his hand on Captain Kidd's booty, either by Kidd entrusting it to him or by "other" means and hid it on the estate. Maybe the ghost of Kidd is looking for his share of the booty. Others say Kidd's wife spirited the booty away long before it made its way to Clermont, yet there are stories of Captain Kidd's booty buried up and down the Hudson. Is Kidd's treasured buried somewhere in the Hudson Valley? Only when someone stumbles upon it will we know for sure. Maybe you will find it.

Visiting Clermont

† Clermont State Historic Site, One Clermont Avenue, Germantown, New York 12526
Phone: 518-537-4240
Website: www.friendsofclermont.org
Email: fofc@gtel.net

Clermont is open May through October. Check the website for dates and times before visiting.

Chapter Nineteen:

Kinderhook

Lindenwald

Lindenwald was the home of Martin Van Buren, the eighth president of the United States. However, the ghostly activity predates the former president. The Van Ness family owned the land originally and Congressman John Peter Van Ness built the mansion, called Kleinrod, in 1797. When Martin Van Buren later purchased the home, he renamed it "Lindenwald," which is Dutch for the linden tree that lines the roads.

William Peter Van Ness, the Congressman's brother, went on to become Kinderhook's first judge. He was also a protégé and close friend of Aaron Burr. If you remember your history, you will recall that Burr, as vice-president,

Lindenwald, Kinderhook... The sounds and smells of cooking emanate from the house's kitchen.

dueled with—and killed—Alexander Hamilton, Secretary of the Treasury. William was the one who communicated Burr's challenge to Hamilton and acted as his second in the fateful duel. According to local legend, the Van Ness' gave Burr refuge in a secret sealed room at Lindenwald after he killed Hamilton. Most people believe it is Burr's ghost that haunts Lindenwald. Whether or not it's Burr, visitors to the home have claimed to see a man, dressed in late eighteenth century clothing, in the yard.

After his tenure as President, Van Buren retired to Lindenwald. He died there in 1862 and was buried in the village cemetery. The President's son, John, inherited Lindenwald. John also inherited his love of politics from his father, but, according to legend, did not inherit a sense of conservatism. John Van Buren loved to gamble, and while gambling, lost his rights to the home to New York City financier, Lawrence Jerome, who brought his family, including his daughter, Jenny, to live at Lindenwald. Jenny Jerome later became the mother of Winston Churchill.

All this lively history makes for a well-haunted house. John reportedly still roams around the house, making stomping noises, slamming doors, and causing other loud crashing noises. Reportedly, a family butler, rejected by his suitor, hung himself in the apple orchard. His body can still be seen on moonlit nights, swinging from a tree limb. Reports have been made of the head cook in the kitchen, still at her task of making the family breakfast, complete with the sound of sizzling and the wafting smell of bacon frying. The first ghost that can make us hungry instead of scared! This house has a full range of ghosts to enjoy.

Visiting Lindenwald

† Lindenwald, 1013 Old Post Road, Kinderhook, New York 12106-3605
Phone: 518-758-9689
Website: www.nps.gov/mava/index/html

The site is open daily mid-May to late October from 9 a.m. to 4 p.m. Guided tours are available.

Part Three:

West Side of the Hudson River

A tugboat chugs down the Hudson. The Hudson was a major water route in early Unites States History.

Near its mouth, Hudson River is 3½ miles wide. Here in the Hudson Valley, we can see both sides of the great river clearly, with towns, cities, mansions, trees, and green mountains along the shoreline. It often seems unbelievable that each side of the Hudson can be so different, but just like the towns and cities, each side of the Hudson has it's own unique history, heritage, character, and energy. Since tradition tells us that spirits cannot cross water, each side of the Hudson also has its own ghosts.

Chapter Twenty:

Bear Mountain

Bear Mountain State Park

Hessian Lake

Hessian Lake is a small lake located inside of Bear Mountain State Park. It is lined with a paved walkway and has benches placed at scenic spots along the walk around the lake. But few people are familiar with Hessian Lake's other name—Bloody Pond. The pond was named after a very bloody Revolutionary battle took place here on October 6, 1777. The British hired

Hessian Lake, Bear Mountain State Park... Headless mounted soldiers ride across the lake.

mercenary soldiers from Germany called "Hessians." They were known as some of the most brutal soldiers in the Revolutionary War, fighting only for money not for honor.

The Patriots, expecting the advancing British, claimed a vantage point just above the pond. If you take a walk around the pond, you will notice how rocky and steep this side of the pond is, but the Patriots were somehow able to get at least one cannon up this seemingly impossible steep, rocky slope. Even though the British and Hessians outnumbered the Patriots, because of this vantage point, they were able to slaughter many advancing soldiers that day. Many of the dead Hessian bodies fell into the pond. The rest of the corpses were collected and thrown in the water with their dead comrades. Eyewitnesses claimed the pond turned red and stayed red afterwards for several days from the Hessian blood. Supposedly, the bodies were never removed from the lake and were allowed to decompose there. Ghostly Hessians are reportedly seen in the lake area, sometimes without their heads. Troops of advancing Hessians are seen charging *over* the lake, as if trying to take the hill. Their ghostly horses gallop over the top of the water, their riders yelling in German. The horse's hooves can be heard striking the rock, as well as the strong grunts of the laboring horses.

Later, in the 1800s, when an ice company started to use Bloody Pond to harvest ice they thought it best to change it's name from Bloody Pond to Highland Pond. Who wants to buy ice taken from a bloody pond? Later, the lake was named Hessian Lake.

Visiting Hessian Lake

† Bear Mountain State Park, Bear Mountain, New York 10911
Phone: 845-786-2701
Website: http://nysparks.state.ny.us/parks/

Bear Mountain State Park is open all year. Sometimes there is a charge for parking on weekends and during special events. For access to the lake, park by the lodge.

Chapter Twenty-One

West Point, New York

West Point Military Academy

When I asked a historian friend, who generally does not believe in ghosts, if West Point was haunted, he replied, "Oh heavens, *everyone* knows that West Point is haunted." There is no doubt a place rich in history could not be haunted. It is rumored that that there are ghosts everywhere at West Point, and if you stay long enough, you are sure to encounter something out of the ordinary. *You can see them in the dormitories, marching across the parade grounds, walking on the tree line paths, visiting the cemetery, and floating through walls.* Some people even claim that you can pass the ghost of a cadet and not even know it because the uniform cadets wear is the same one they have worn for over a century.

Thomas Jefferson signed legislation establishing the United States Military Academy in 1802. This makes West Point the longest continuously running military academy of its kind in the United States. However, the history of West Point goes back much further. West Point played a crucial role in the Revolutionary War. Fort Putman, named after Israel Putnam, a heroic General in the American Revolutionary War, is located on the grounds of West Point, on a hilltop. It's open to the public in the summer. Shadowy figures have been "seen" at Fort Putnam and people have reported the sound of "shuffling" footsteps when there is no one else around.

Fort Arnold, formerly located where the current parade grounds are, was named after Benedict Arnold. America's best-known traitor tried to surrender West Point to the British, but was unsuccessful. In July of 1780, Arnold was given command of West Point. His plan had been to hand over this strategic location to the British, but the plan was foiled when the Americans captured British Major John André, who was carrying the plans for the traitorous act. André was hanged as a spy, but Arnold narrowly escaped capture and went on to serve in the British Army. It should come as no surprise then that the ghost of a man bearing Arnold's likeness has been seen striding quickly across the parade grounds, the former Fort Arnold, deep in thought. He then *disappears* into the shadows. I have no doubt it is Arnold, perhaps reconsidering the decision he made over two centuries ago or perhaps he is on the way to the *Vulture,* anchored in the Hudson, on which he will make his escape.

It is from West Point, known then as Trophy Point, where the famous chain was stretched across the Hudson River to stop the advancing British ships. The chain was hung, in the water, across the narrowest part of the river from Trophy Point to Constitution Island. Reports have been made that late at night you can hear the call of soldiers on the water carefully guiding the chain across the Hudson.

The most noisy and boisterous ghost at West Point is located in the Superintendent's House. It seems a young maid named Molly, who worked in the house, still remains there and she is known to poke people, move things, and pull the covers off sleeping visitors to the home. The Superintendent's House is a private residence.

The large barracks located in the center of the campus are also haunted. Many young cadets have been shocked by the image of a nineteenth century era cadet standing in their rooms. Ghosts of long dead cadets, as well as Revolutionary War soldiers, are known to wander the grounds at night and appear to *walk through* solid stone walls.

West Point Cemetery

The West Point Cemetery is also haunted, as most cemeteries are. Overlooking the Hudson River, the cemetery was originally the burying grounds for local inhabitants and Revolutionary soldiers. The oldest grave dates back to 1782 and belongs to Dominick Trant, an ensign in the Ninth Massachusetts Infantry. The grounds were designated a military cemetery in 1817 for West Point's honored dead and their families. A caretaker's cottage, erected in 1872, now serves as a visitors' center. The cemetery is opened during daylight hours and if you stop at the caretaker's cottage, you can pick up a self-guided walking tour of the cemetery. Many famous soldiers—from all the American wars—can be found buried here. Make sure you also visit the grave of General Egbert L. Viele and his wife, Juliette Dana Viele. You will not need a map to find this grave. The pyramid, complete with two sphinxes guarding the doorway, is visible from just about anywhere

in the graveyard. Don't miss General George Armstrong Custer's grave nearby. Shadowy figures and orbs of lights have been seen inside the cemetery.

West Point offers guided tours, but before you visit, you should call ahead to the visitor center to ensure the grounds will be open on the day of your visit. There is also a museum located at the visitor's center.

Visiting West Point

† West Point Visitor's Center
Phone: 845-938-2638
Website: www.usma.edu

~~~

† West Point Tours
Phone: 845-446-4724
Website: www.westpointtours
Email: westpointtours@hvc.rr.com

General Egbert L. Viele's grave in the cemetery at West Point Military Academy is complete with sphinxes at the doorway and the remnants of gold gilt inside.

It is important to keep in mind that West Point is a military installation. You cannot just "walk around." You must carefully watch signs. Visitors are only allowed in many areas of the campus when accompanied by a cadet. Other areas are restricted. You are also allowed to visit the cemetery and Fort Putnam on your own. Every person visiting West Point must provide a photo ID. Visitors' cars will also be searched prior to entry onto the base; obviously, don't bring weapons of any sort. It is best to call ahead since West Point hosts concerts, footballs games, and all types of ceremonies, and the base can be overwhelmingly crowded. Others times, its very quiet and…well, haunted.

~~~~~

Storm King Pass

What is a haunted site without a madman? Anthony Wayne, Revolutionary War general, was born in 1745. In his civilian life, he was a tanner, land surveyor, and a strong patriot for the American cause. When the war began, he quickly raised a militia eager to fight for the cause of the patriots.

Storm King Mountain… "Mad" Anthony Wayne and his faithful horse, Nab, ride over this mountain. Flames shoot from Nab's nostrils and hooves, leaving in the surrounding air a strong smell of sulfur.

"Mad" Anthony Wayne is best known in the Hudson Valley for his courageous midnight attack of Stony Point on July 16, 1779. In this attack, the soldiers' only weapon was the bayonet. Reportedly, the assault lasted only thirty minutes against the British — the Patriots had managed to sneak up on the heavily fortified British and overtake the fort without firing a single shot.

"Mad" Anthony Wayne reportedly got his nickname from two sources. The first is he had a facial tick, which gave him an unnerving appearance. He was also known for his courageous war efforts that seemed crazy to some people. Besides his gun-less siege at Stony Point, he is also known for his courageous ride over Storm King Mountain. Viewed from the Hudson, Storm King Mountain rises up clear and steep. It is mostly rock with little vegetation. When compared to the adjoining mountains it looks gray and "bald." Impossible to traverse, there is no development on this mountain to this day. The terrain is too rocky and steep. The narrow winding road along the edge of the mountain did not exist in Wayne's day. "Mad" Anthony Wayne is said to have ridden over the mountain, at full speed, to warn the American Revolutionary soldiers of an impending attack by the British. Reports are that on nights just before a storm, "Mad" Anthony Wayne and his horse, Nab, reenact this ride. Sparks shoot from the horse's hooves as they strike the rock and fire shoots from the horse's nostrils. The horse's hooves striking the rock and the flames from his nose leave a strong smell of sulfur in the air. Wayne can be heard shouting, urging his horse on. Just before they reach the crest of the mountain, they will disappear.

If you want to see if you can hear Wayne and Nab, take a drive down the winding Storm King Highway, also called Route 218. It is a short and scenic drive. The road is only ten miles long. It runs from Cornwall-on-Hudson to the West Point Military Academy. There was no road access to Storm King Mountain until the early 1900s. The road we can ride on today was opened in 1922. As you drive, you will see why the ride by Mad Anthony Wayne was seen as both heroic and mad. Please note that due to its narrow, winding, and rocky nature, it is often closed during the winter months. The roadway also experiences rockslides, so you should be aware of the possibility of rocks on the roadway.

Visiting Storm King Mountain and Route 218

† From USMA at West Point, exit via Lee Gate to drive on Route 218.

You will probably want to drive the route more than once. There is limited parking on the road, so early morning is best if you want to stop and try collecting EVPs or photographs.

Chapter Twenty-Two:
Cornwall-on-Hudson

Moodna Creek
(Moodua Creek)

Moodna Creek, 15.5 miles long, is the longest creek located totally within Orange County. It empties into the Hudson River. Moodna is a corruption of the Dutch word "murderers," for it was on this creek that the entire Stacy family met their demise.

In the late 1600s, the Stacy family built a log cabin near the mouth of Moodna Creek. They were a good, hard-working Christian family. They were befriended by a local Native American named Naoman, who visited the family quite often and was particularly fond of the children. He would bring them little gifts each time he visited. Naoman spent many evenings

The mouth of Moodna Creek, Cornwall... Mrs. Stacy wanders, searching for her murdered children.

around the Stacy's family hearth, but one evening when he visited the family noticed a change in his demeanor. At the same time, the children had found some strange talisman in the woods near their house. They had found an arrowhead wrapped in snakeskin and from the tip hung a crow's feather. Later, they also found a tomahawk hanging above the family's door. The family questioned Naoman and he said he would only tell them what these signs meant if they swore to absolutely secrecy and then heeded his words. The family told Naoman that they considered him family and would take any secret he told them to the grave. Naoman told them that some of the local Native Americans had grievances with some white people and, as revenge, planned to kill all the white settlers in the area. Naoman pleaded with the family to flee for their lives. The family didn't need to be warned twice—they immediately packed what they could and fled to the Hudson River. Little did Naoman know he had sent the Stacys into a trap.

Just as the family's small boat neared Pollopel Island (now called Bannerman Island), they were met by a large canoe with a dozen strong warriors waiting for any fleeing white settlers. The Stacys were captured and brought back to the Native American council. Mrs. Stacy was handled very roughly by the Native Americans, who thought she would be the easiest to break under pressure. The Native Americans demanded that she tell them who had betrayed them and warned the Stacys of the imminent attack. But true to their word, none of the Stacys would give up the name of their dear friend.

The Stacy children were brought in front of their mother. The Native American chief said he would slay the children right in front of her if she did not give up the name. Still, she remained silent. The tomahawk was raised above the children's head when finally Naoman yelled for the chief to stop. He had never seen such loyalty in friends before and could not bear to see his good friends murdered in front of him. He went to the middle of the council circle, admitted to the deed, and knelt down to be killed. Naoman was felled by several blows to the head, but his confession did not save the Stacy family. After Naoman was savagely slaughtered, the entire Stacy family was also slaughtered.

When innocent people are killed, often times their spirits linger on and so it is with the Stacy family. The ghost of Mrs. Stacy has been seen walking the shores of the Hudson near the mouth of Moodna Creek searching for her children. You can hear her crying and wailing before she disappears.

Visiting Moodna Creek

† Moodna Creek feeds into the Hudson River near Cornwall-on-Hudson. Follow Shore Road off of 9W.

Chapter Twenty-Three:

Glenham, New York

Bannerman Island

I first saw Bannerman Island, like many people, on a train ride to New York City. The ruins of a castle, looking strangely medieval and out of place, are seen just off the east coast of the Hudson River. Originally called Pollopel, the island is just slightly larger than six acres. Native Americans believed this small island was already haunted before white settlers arrived in the New World. Archeological excavations done on the island prove that there was no early settlement prior to Mr. Bannerman. Something about the island kept Native Americans from putting any sort

Bannerman Island... Passersby claim to hear strange whistles and noises from this island.

of permanent site on it—Native Americans would not inhabit a place they believed was haunted. The Dutch also believed the island was inhabited by *other worldly* creatures and built no permanent buildings there. The island was left undeveloped and uninhabited until 1900.

The Dutch name for the island was "Potlepel Eylant," which translates from Dutch to "Pot Ladle" Island. (Later the name became Pollopel Island.) A pot ladle is the large ladle you often seen in colonial museums positioned next to the fireplace. "Potladle" is pejorative for "drunkard" because when a sailor was drunk he was said to be "dunked in the stew." Since the island was thought to be enchanted, most likely by evil spirits, early Dutch sailors left drunken mates on the island until they sobered up. Hopefully, the fear of being on this strange, enchanted island would scare the sailors enough to refrain from drinking to excess in the future. Reports came from many newly sobered sailors of "goblin like" creatures haunting the island. Perhaps this is where Henry Hudson met up with the "little men" described as "pig-like." To protect themselves from these "evil spirits," the sailors believed that each new sailor had to be dunked in the water as they passed the island for the first time. This is very similar to the dunking new sailors receive when crossing the equator for the first time.

Also, according to the Dutch, a ship wrecked in a storm just off the west shore of the island and they claim that on stormy nights, as they approached the island, they could hear the captain yelling orders to his crew.

Bannerman Island is not haunted in the traditional sense; that is, it is not haunted by people who have died there. Rather, it is haunted by spirits that are considered "other worldly." The Native Americans believed it was the earth itself that was haunted. Strange noises, high pitched whistling, and sounds of humans shouting have been reported on the island. Legend says that no man would be able to inhabit the island and, if he did, his house would be destroyed. This legend seems to have borne itself out.

Whether Francis Bannerman heard these rumors or not, he decided to purchase the island in 1900 to store munitions. He ran a military surplus business and needed a safe place to secure rounds of ammunition. He renamed the island after himself, Bannerman Island, and decided to build a large castle that would be the storehouse for his business and a summer home for his family. The elaborate castle was entirely designed by Bannerman and took seventeen years to complete. A collector and dealer, the island fortress came to store some of the country's finest war relics, such as the chain placed across the Hudson during the Revolutionary War, a table owned by George Washington, and equipment used by Admiral Perry on his Arctic Expedition. These were donated to the Smithsonian Institute in Washington, D.C. after the state of New York purchased the island from the Bannerman family in 1967. Bannerman Island also had extensive gardens, a family mansion, and many outbuildings.

As often with gunpowder, there were several accidents on the island, the largest occurring in 1920. The blast was so devastating it blew debris onto the mainland, obstructing the train tracks on the east side of the river. Several men were killed in the blast. However, the business was able to recover. The family finally sold the island to the state of New York. They had not resided on the island in a long time and no longer used it for business interests. The state had planned to renovate the island and open it to visitors, but in 1969, the castle was destroyed by fire. Though the fire was suspicious in nature, no cause was ever determined. Some say it was the spirits claiming back their island. Since the island was known to have stored large amounts of gunpowder, firefighters were not allowed on the island to put out the fire. Instead, they stood guard as the buildings were ravaged. The island has remained off limits from that time until 1994, when the Bannerman Castle Trust took over the island.

The ghosts of Bannerman Island have been heard and photographed. Images of floating orbs or human shaped shadows have been seen and photographed by visitors. Many people have photographed mists, some in human form, all over the island. Also, visitors have heard sounds of strange noises. There are still reports of odd clicking sounds, whistling, and the sound of indistinguishable voices. In the evening, the sound of galloping horses can be heard. A friend of mine describes Bannerman Island as a "festival of spirits." Bannerman Island is open for visitations. Make sure you bring a camera. Tours are only available in the summer and autumn months. Kayak tours are also available.

Visiting Bannerman Island

† Island Tours:

Tours, available from May to October, leave from the Torches Restaurant dock in Newburgh. For information or reservations, call 845-220-2120.

Website: www.bannermancastle.org

~~~

† Kayak Tours:

Tours are available from both Cold Spring and Cornwall. For reservations and information about kayak tours from Cold Spring, call 845-265-0221; for reservations and information about kayak tours from Cornwall, call 845-534-7800.

Website: HudsonValleyOutfitters.com

Chapter Twenty-Four:

Newburgh, New York

Danskammer Point

Danskammer Point is a place on the Hudson just two miles north of Newburgh. It projects out into the Hudson River. After a shipping accident, a lighthouse was built there in 1886 to warn passing ships. However, in earlier times, Danskammer Point was called Duyvil's Danskammer, which is Dutch for "devil's dance chamber," named by early Dutch settlers who observed that Native Americans met there for ceremonial dances. Native Americans would gather at this site, dancing and drumming all night long. To the Dutch, these ceremonies of wild dancing, loud drumming, fire jumping, and loud screaming and shouting was terrifying. Never experiencing a divergently different culture, the Dutch misinterpreted these Native American rituals as "satanic." The Native Americans urged the white settlers to mind their own business and not even attempt to attend these ceremonies. White settlers who were caught in the area were often taken prisoner, tortured, and ransomed.

Danskammer Point now holds the Dynergy Power Plant, but many say the spirits of the Native Americans have not left this sacred meeting place. On very dark nights, the Native American spirits are said to, once again, build their fires and perform ancient rituals. People have claimed to see these council fires and hear the whoops of the Native Americans dancing around them.

Visiting Danskammer Point

† From 9W, drive down River Road
You can no longer visit the actual point itself. Be careful if you decide to park, the road is very narrow and winding. Definitely, there is haunted energy in this area.

Chapter Twenty-Five:

Highland

Highland Public Library

In 1929, the Georgianna Rose Ganse Foundation generously offered Highland Library use of Dr. Caspar Ganse's former home. This offered allowed the library to move in, rent free, as long as they maintained the building. The library opened at this location in 1930. In 1973, the building was donated to the Highland Free Library. The library has renovated over the years, growing to meet the demands of the town's readers.

Highland Public Library, Highland... The previous owner still wanders the aisles, keeping an eye on things and making sure the shelves are in order.

However, it would seem that Dr. Ganse has decided to stay on in his old home. There are reports of books moving, doors opening and closing on their own, and a figure of a man, supposedly Dr. Ganse, has been seen all over the library. If you visit the library, keep an eye out for him.

Visiting Highland Public Library

† Highland Public Library, 30 Church Street, Highland, New York 12528

Phone: 845-691-2275

Website: http://www.highlandlibrary.org

~~~~~

Mid-Hudson Bridge

Connecting Poughkeepsie and Highland

Until the 1920s there was only one bridge across the river in the Hudson Valley and it was located at Bear Mountain. The next bridge, far to the north, was in Albany. Automobiles were quickly becoming the main mode of

Mid-Hudson Bridge connecting Highland with Poughkeepsie... Former workers still can be seen at their posts.

transportation and, without the bridges, travelers had to rely on ferryboats, many of which were ill-equipped for transporting cars across the Hudson. In the Mid-Hudson, there arose a dire need for bridges.

The cornerstone of the Mid-Hudson Bridge was laid October 9, 1925. Many unexpected delays took place; as a result, the bridge did not open until August 25, 1930. Several workmen died on the project and it's their restless spirits that are said to haunt the bridge at night. Some claim to see them up in the suspension lines or, along with other ghosts, walking on the pedestrian walkway.

While on the Mid-Hudson Bridge, you will notice the Poughkeepsie Railroad Bridge. Before the Mid-Hudson Bridge was built, the main way for people to cross the river was by railway on this bridge. When this bridge was completed in 1888, it was the longest bridge in the world. It has been closed since 1974. Plans to rebuild it as a pedestrian bridge are underway. Reports are this bridge is also haunted. I can't wait until it opens to do some investigations!

Visiting the Mid-Hudson Bridge

† Visit the Mid-Hudson Bridge and walk across the pedestrian path. I recommend visiting from the Highland side of the bridge. There is parking in Johnson-Iorio Memorial Park on Haviland Road (off of 9W). From the park, there are great views of the Hudson, as well as both bridges.

~~~~~

Pang Yang

It's difficult to get to the source of the story of Gray Lady and Pang Yang. As I researched and unraveled each fanciful story, it seems that two myths have been woven into one and have become a Gordian knot to unravel. Somehow, the story of the prophetess Jemima Wilkinson and the mysterious people of Pang Yang have been knit into one single story. I will tell the story as it was told to me by several sources. However, I hope you can help me solve this mystery

Jemima Wilkinson was born a Quaker in Rhode Island in 1765. In 1776, Jemima suffered a high fever and slipped into a coma. Not having the medical ability to determine if Jemima was still alive—that she had most likely fallen into a coma—her family prepared for her funeral. On the morning of her burial, her mother wanted to take one last look at her beloved daughter. Much to their surprise, when the coffin was pried open, Jemima Wilkinson sat up and began to speak! She claimed that the spirit of Jemima Wilkinson had left her for heaven and a new spirit

inhabited her body. This new spirit was known as the Publick Universal Friend. Jemima started a new religion based on her near-death visions. After several years of preaching, she sought a permanent home for her growing religion. She and her followers set up a religious community in upstate New York near the community of Penn Yann, which she called Jerusalem. According to local Hudson Valley legend, a small group of her followers, around the year 1800, established a religious community known as Pang Yang between what is now New Paltz and Highland. These believers were originally headed west to join Wilkinson; however, after crossing the Hudson, they took a liking to the area and decided to stay.

Before her death in 1819, Wilkinson made a pledge to her followers and their descendants that she would take visible form just before each of them died to comfort and help the dying person "pass over." True to her word, there have been many sightings of the "Gray Lady," so called, because the specter is dressed head-to-toe in gray, similar to the Quakers' plain dress. According to a local historian, a woman named Carolyn Calhoon, one of the members of the Pang Yang Community, would see the "Gray Lady" within twelve hours of the death of any community member. Soon after, other members of the community also claimed to see their spiritual leader. There are conflicting reports of how long the community lasted as a cohesive community in Ulster County. Claims of Pang Yangers still living in the hills were reported as late as the 1950s. To this day local people claim to see a woman in gray appear shortly before a death. Some people are unaware that an ancestor may have had an affiliation with the Pang Yang community until the Gray Lady appears. It seems Jemima intends to keep her promise.

I have found no historical link between the Pang Yang community in Ulster County and Jemima Wilkinson's community, Jerusalem, outside of Penn Yann, New York. However, that story persists. It seems the true Pang Yangers were not followers of Jemima Wilkinson at all. However, their past is more mysterious than the prophetess who appears to them.

I spoke to one man who actually met one of the last Pang Yangers of Ulster County. I also met with the historian for the town of Lloyd; he showed me pictures of the Pang Yangers in their homes. These were not the soft-spoken, simple descendants of Quakers. They were rough-cut mountain people, most likely a mix between freed and runaway slaves,

Opposite page, top:
Homemade sign marks the Pang Yang Cemetery, Highland.

Opposite page, bottom:
Pang Yang Cemetery, Highland... Unmarked stones strewn down hill. The origins of these strange people is still a mystery.

Native Americans, and rough neck white settlers. How they came to settle in Ulster County is an ongoing mystery. They were largely illiterate and worked as laborers. They built huts out of oilcans and lived very rustically.

So, who exactly is this Gray Lady who appears to the descendants of the Pang Yangers?

The Pang Yang Community was located on Lily Lake Road just off Route 299 outside of New Paltz. The Pang Yang Cemetery is marked with a plain wooden marker. The graves are roughly marked with upright fieldstone with no engraving. I doubt the stones mark actual burials. When I visited the graveyard for the first time, I noticed that several stones were marked with American flags. I thought, finally, a solution to my riddle! I could find out who was in at least one of these graves and find his family. However, when I asked about the flag marked gravestones, I was told that there was an "assumption" that at least several Pang Yangers had served their country so they marked several random graves!

Who were these people? Where did they come from? Who is the Gray Lady that appears to them? Maybe you can help me solve these mysteries!

Visiting Pang Yang

† Take Lily Lake Road just off Route 299 outside of New Paltz. This is where the community of Pang Yang was located. Pull into the driveway of the town's transfer station and park. *(Please park all the way off this road as it is very winding and dangerous.)* Just across the street from the transfer station, is the Pang Yang cemetery. Visit the graveyard in late fall, before the first snow or in the summer months. Any other time of the year, you risk the ground being too muddy to get up the hill. It is located on private property, so stay on the path up to the cemetery.

Chapter Twenty-Six:

New Paltz

Elting Memorial Library

Elting Memorial Library is housed in an old Dutch stone building originally called the Phillip LeFevre Elting House. The library purchased the house in 1920. Oddly enough, there are no records as to when this house was built and by whom. There are suggestions that it was built as early as 1740 and as late as 1824. Solomon Elting is the first recorded owner in the early 1800s. It was used as both a general store and a residence. Phillip LeFevre Elting purchased the house in 1919 for $4,000 with the purpose of donating it to the town as a library. Hence, the library bears his name, though he never took up residency in the house.

The old section of the library definitely creeks and has the feel of a haunted library. Many people claim to hear unexplained creaking sounds, like a person would make by walking, when no one is around. In addition, people have reported feeling a "presence" or "being watched."

Elting Memorial Library, New Paltz... A security camera captured a shadowy image walking around inside the building.

In October 2007, an image of a ghost was recorded on the library's security cameras. A librarian arriving to open the library for the day discovered an outside door left ajar. Fearing that someone had broken into the library, he reviewed tape from the security camera of the night before. To his surprise, at 3:30 a.m., a mysterious ghost-like figure is seen moving around the room before it finally vanishes out the door. So far, no one has any explanation for the door being left open and the ghostly figure. Perhaps it's Solomon Elting just visiting to see all the great things the library is doing with his former home.

Visiting Elting Memorial Library

† Elting Memorial Library, 93 Main Street, New Paltz, New York 12561

Phone: 845-255-5030

Website: http://elting.newpaltz.lib.ny.us/

Email: newpaltzeltinglibrary@yahoo.com

~~~~~

Huguenot Street

Everyone has his or her favorite haunted place and Huguenot Street is mine. Every time I visit, I am never disappointed. The spirits are always active, warm, and welcoming.

In 1677, twelve French Huguenots purchased 40,000 acres along the Wallkill River from the Esopus Native Americans. They settled in this area to practice their Protestant faith free from persecution. The solid stone homes they built on the shores of the Wallkill River are still standing, now preserved and open to the public. Huguenot Street, later named after the Huguenots who settled there, is one of the oldest continuously inhabited streets in the United States. The street has six stone houses, a replica church, and the original graveyard. Most people think of the American South when they think of slavery. However, slavery was once practiced actively in New York and Huguenot Street is one of the places where you can see households in which slaves played an active role.

Huguenot Street is not just a collection of old houses; it is a living history museum. Along with maintaining the historic houses and opening them for tours, the museum maintains an archive of documents relating to the history of the street, its inhabitants, their descendants and the local area.

~~~~~~~~

The Freer House

The best place to start your ghostly visit is at the Freer House located on the corner of Huguenot Street and Broadhead Avenue. Hugo Freer, one of the original twelve French Huguenots, built it most likely in the 1600s or early 1700s. Annie Dubois owned the house in the 1930s. She rented it out and lived next door in a newer structure. Ironically, the house was rented to a descendant of the original owner and he was also named Hugo Freer, after his ancestor. Annie was a bit of a spinster, never marrying. She had fallen in love with Hugo Freer, even though he was quite a bit younger than she was. A close bond developed between the two. However, Annie kept her true feelings for Hugo a secret. Hugo fell ill suddenly and was rushed to Kingston City Hospital, the nearest hospital in those days, and died of appendicitis. News soon reached the village of Hugo's death. Annie went missing the very night that Hugo died. Being a small town, Annie's disappearance was noticed almost immediately and large search parties went out to look for her. Annie could not be found anywhere. Near dawn, a group of searchers decided to take a second look at the land surrounding the rental home. Now that the sun was up, searchers could see down the large well next to the house. When they peered down into the well, they

Freer House, Huguenot Street, New Paltz... Annie Dubois, grief-stricken over the death of the man she loved, threw herself to her death in the house's well.

The well in which Annie drowned herself.

could see Annie where she had flung herself in grief over her beloved. Though never joined in life, Annie and Hugo were buried on the same day in the New Paltz rural cemetery where they still repose today. People have claimed to see Annie's restless spirit still walking on Huguenot Street... perhaps in search of her beloved.

Abraham Hasbrouck House

The ghost most seen on Huguenot Street appears at the Abraham Hasbrouck House, right next door to the Freer House. A tall, slender man dressed in black is seen leaving and entering the house with a dog. This dark specter carries an axe over his shoulder. People who have seen him enter the house have noted that he leaves no footprints, even in snow. The most frightening account of the "Axe Man" is a report that he was seen in the upstairs window, making vicious chopping motions with his axe. To look into this window, look up just left of the chimney as you face the side of the house. No one has been able to figure out what he is "chopping." Maybe you can.

The Evers inhabited the Hasbrouck House in the early 1900s. Alf Evers was a famous local historian. His mother considered herself a psychic. For years, she claimed that there was a body buried in the basement. To appease his wife, Mr. Evers, during renovations, dug up the basement floor

Abraham Hasbrouck House, Huguenot Street, New Paltz.... A ghostly specter of a man all dressed in black has been seen entering and exiting this house.

Side view, Abraham Hasbrouck House, Huguenot Street, New Paltz... The specter, dressed in all black, has been seen in this window viciously chopping something with an axe.

and, much to his surprise, he did, indeed, find a small skeleton buried there. He took the skeleton and laid it out on an upstairs table and invited friends and neighbors to come and examine it. However, over the next few days the disinterred skeleton, exposed to air after all those years, disintegrated and turned to dust leaving the skeleton in the basement a mystery.

The Dubois Fort

The Dubois Fort, now the gift shop run by the museum, is located in the center of Huguenot Street. It has always been a meeting place for people and continues to be to this day. Elsie Oates was one of the former owners in the 1940s and ran a restaurant at the location. She lived upstairs from the business. One night she claimed to see the apparition of a well-dressed Victorian woman. She wore a beautiful brown dress, white collar, and the outfit was completed by a beautiful brown velvet ribbon around the apparition's neck. The only thing missing was...the apparition's head! Fifty years later, the same ghost can still be seen. To this day, staff operating the gift shop will report hearing noises in adjacent rooms and, when they go to check on the source of the noises, they catch a glimpse of the corner of a brown skirt leaving the room. Reports of the headless woman also come from the street itself. People have reported seeing a headless woman floating up the street in the exactly the same outfit that Elsie Oates reported. Perhaps she is whom we see the tall black man chopping in the house across the street!

I have visited Huguenot Street many times. Though I have felt many energies and spirits, I had never seen any physical manifestations until I went one day to take photographs. It was late spring and it was an unusually hot and humid weekday. There were very few people visiting Huguenot Street and most of the late morning, I wandered up and down

Dubois Fort, Huguenot Street, New Paltz... The ghost of a well-dressed headless woman still wanders the rooms.

the street taking pictures. I decided to take several shots of the front of the fort. Holding my digital camera up, I clearly saw a person walking across the front porch of the fort. Not wanting this person in my picture, I lifted my head to wait for her to cross. Much to my surprise, when I looked up, there was no one there! I had caught a glimpse of some ghostly figure, though she appeared to have her head intact. Who she was I'll never know because I didn't snap the picture!

The Deyo House

Moving further down Huguenot Street, the Deyo House is a renovated stone house. Due to these renovations, the home appears very different from the other homes on the street. In 1894, Judge Abraham Brodhead and his wife, Margaret, were involved in an extensive renovation of the house and built a large Queen Anne style addition. The house is barely recognizable as an "old stone house." This house is known for its "bad luck," poltergeist activity, and hauntings.

Deyo House, Huguenot Street, New Paltz... This house is known for its poltergeist activities, particularly pictures that move of their own volition.

Abraham and Margaret had a daughter, Gertrude, who was quite sickly. Their daughter died after giving birth to her first child. Portraits of each of these three early owners—the Judge, Margaret, and Gertrude—hang in the house. Originally, all three portraits hung on the top floor. When museum restorations began on the house, the pictures of the Judge and his wife were moved downstairs to the front hall. Due to lack of space on the downstairs wall, the daughter's picture was left in its original spot on the top floor. However, Gertrude's picture would not stay on the wall upstairs! Staff, arriving in the morning, would find the picture on the floor, with all its hardware intact. Finally, when the picture was found fifteen feet from where it originally hung, staff decided to move Gertrude downstairs to join her parents. Though her picture does not hang in the same room with her parents, the picture seems to be close enough to keep Gertrude on the wall.

Staff have reported other pictures moving, repeatedly, throughout the day, saying that they will leave a room, return shortly after, and find pictures rearranged. This is usually preceded by the sound of doors closing and footsteps. Staff in the kitchen have reported seeing a woman climbing the servant's staircase. Chasing after the figure, they find no one there when they reach the second floor.

After Gertrude, the Judge and his wife never had more children. They lost the house and their fortune to bankruptcy. The next owner also was unable to conceive children and lost the house to bankruptcy. The following owner also could not conceive children. Some people believe there is a haunted curse on the home. It very well could be.

In the mid-1900, during an update of the yard, a worker was putting up a fence. As he dug a post, he came across some old bones. An excavation was done and it was discovered to be a Native American grave. The house had been built on a Native American burial ground! Everyone knows that building on the site of an old graveyard could very well cause a house to be haunted—and every staff member who I have spoken with about the Deyo House had his or her own haunted story to tell me.

The LeFevre House

Further down the road is the LeFevre House. This house has a brick Georgian front, making it look more "modern" than the other houses. This house reflects the "changing times" on Huguenot Street from the colonial era to the birth of a new and thriving nation. According to a letter by William Heidgerd to the New York Historical Society, ghosts from the adjacent cemetery would "visit" him and his family in the house. They claim that they became familiar with their ghost family. Also, he claimed that the family could differentiate the ghostly callers by the sounds each individual specter made.

Another of my personal ghostly experiences happened in the LeFevre House. Though I had visited Huguenot Street many times, it had always been during the day. This time, I was visiting at night, on Halloween, of all nights. The museum staff, keeping with the holiday spirit, had arranged the front parlor of the LeFevre House as an early 1800s wake. A small coffin had been laid out across two saw-horses. The tables had been pushed back and chairs arranged around the room for callers. When I arrived in the house as part of a tour, the spirit of a woman in early 1800s garb greeted

LeFevre House, Huguenot Street, New Paltz... The spirits of the neighboring graveyard visit this house on a regular basis.

us. She had on a black dress and a small white lace piece on her head and a starched white collar. She seemed agitated, as one who had just been visited by death, and a little uneasy about having so many "guests" in her house. Only I could sense her presence, but those with me reported feeling a "cold chill" when they walked in the room and one person claimed he felt the hair stand up straight on the back of his neck. I do not know who this woman was, but she was clearly dressed for mourning, as the appearance of a coffin in her parlor, had most likely attracted her energy to this place. I wonder if she was a specter from the adjoining cemetery or a former mistress of the house.

The Old Burying Ground

Next to the LeFevre house is the original burying ground. Graves date back to the 1600s, though marked graves only date to the early 1700s. The church in the yard is a replica of the original stone church. Before the houses were owned by the museum, owners of the LeFevre house claimed that "tenants" of the graveyard would visit them at night. This old graveyard is haunted by shadowy figures and orbs of light.

Old Burying Ground, Huguenot Street, New Paltz... Orbs of lights have been seen levitating around the cemetery.

The Jacob Hasbrouck House

The last house is the Jacob Hasbrouck House. It is up on the little hill and is the most imposing house of the old street. The front room of this house was used as a tavern and general store. Past tenants of this house report hearing someone walking around in the attic. Each time the tenant climbed the attic stairs and pushed open the attic door, she found no one there. One tenet's dog was afraid to go into a certain area of the back of the attic. The dog would lie at the top of the attic stairs and stubbornly refuse to follow its owner into the attic. The same tenant had a late night "chat" with the ghost and, supposedly, the ghost quieted down for a while.

Not all the ghosts on Huguenot Street are from a distant historic past. One of the office buildings on Huguenot Street is said to be haunted by a past employee who promised to come back after his death to the place he loved so much. The coat closet where this employee hung his jacket each day will open on its own. Employees report closing the door and minutes

Hasbrouck House, Huguenot Street, New Paltz... The attic is haunted by a noisy spirit.

later returning and finding the door open again. Employees also report checking this door before they leave at night and finding it open the next day. Occasionally, they will hear footsteps. They've come to accept it is just their beloved co-worker still at his job.

Though the houses are only accessible by guided tour, Huguenot Street is a public street. You can walk up and down anytime you wish. I visit Huguenot Street all the time for some informal ghost hunting. If you are ghost hunting after dark, please be quiet, as many homes on Huguenot Street are privately owned. Respect the residents. Also, use your common sense and do not visit any place alone after dark.

Visiting Huguenot Street

† Huguenot Street, 18 Broadhead Avenue, New Paltz, New York 12561
Phone: 845-255-1660
Website: ww.hhs-newpaltz.org

Huguenot Street is located off route 299 and runs along the Wallkill River. The museum maintains a free parking lot at 18 Broadhead Avenue. The visitor center is located at the Dubois Fort.

I strongly recommend that you take a tour and get to know the "lay of the land." However, Huguenot Street is a public street. You may park and just enjoy a stroll up and down the street at any time of the day. Each house is marked with a historic marker giving you basic information about the house. You can only access the inside of the houses via a guided tour with the exception of the Dubois Fort, which has a gift shop that is open to the public. Tours are available May through October. There are special haunted tours around Halloween, which I also highly recommend. You must make a reservation to take the Halloween tour, as they are often sold out.

~~~~~

New Paltz Rural Cemetery

I don't believe there is a cemetery that does not have spiritual activity. Though I have heard no formal ghost stories about the New Paltz Rural Cemetery, I did receive confirmation from the *spirit world* that the spirits are active in this cemetery.

The New Paltz Rural Cemetery was chartered in 1861. The previous small family and church cemeteries were inadequate to handle the growing population of the area. Plus, many families lost a loved ones during the Civil War, making it necessary to expand existing burial grounds. The New Paltz Rural Cemetery covers thirty-two acres and has more than 6,500 graves. There is room for at least that many more. It is a very peaceful cemetery set in a lovely rural setting with views of the Shawangunk Ridge and away from the hustle and bustle of the main roads.

One late fall day, a friend of mine and I were out taking pictures of haunted and historic places. It was mid-December and quite cold. The day was gray and overcast and, by 3 o'clock, it was becoming too dark to take pictures. On a whim, we decided to look for Annie M. Dubois and Hugo Freer's gravesites, the two residents of Huguenot Street who died on the same day. *(See their story under the Huguenot Street, Freer House, listing.)* At first, we actually went to the wrong cemetery. After consulting a map, we found the New Paltz Rural Cemetery. Both Freer and Dubois are common names in this area, plus with the cold and waning light, we did not really believe we'd find the graves. We started in the older section of the graveyard, believing this would be the best place to start. We would drive, stop when we saw either surname, and hop out and look to see if it was one of the graves we were searching for. Anyone who has ever tried to find a grave knows this is a very ineffective way to do so. We stopped in the far corner of the graveyard. It was cold and almost dark.

We figured it was time to head home when I said simply, "You know, we haven't asked them yet." Looking out across the stones, I said, "Annie, Hugo, we'd really like to find your stones so I can have a picture for this book." In less than a few minutes, we had driven across the graveyard and were standing at the gravestone of Annie M. Dubois. Could it really be the Annie M we were looking for? After all, I figured Annie might be a common name, though this one was the only one we had seen thus far in our search. We snapped pictures and I noted the date. "Ok, Hugo," I said, "You're next." Just a moment later, one row down, we were standing at the foot of Hugo's grave. The confirmation that we were at the right graves were the same death dates. I have absolutely no doubt it was Annie who led us directly to those graves. We left a stone at each grave and thanked our help from the other side.

The graves of Annie Dubois and Hugo Freer, New Paltz Rural Cemetery... Annie Dubois killed herself by throwing herself in a well upon hearing of the death of her beloved, Hugo Freer. Yet Freer, who died suddenly of appendicitis, never knew she loved him. They were buried on the same day a short distance from each other.

Visiting the New Paltz Rural Cemetery

> † New Paltz Cemetery, 81 Plains Road, New Paltz, New York 12561
> Phone: 845-255-0835
> Website: www.newpaltzruralcemetery.com

Both Annie's and Hugo's graves can be found on the left side of the cemetery as you enter. The rows are not numbered.

When pulling into the cemetery you will see a lone grave standing oddly in the middle of the empty burying ground on your right. This is the stone of boxing legend Floyd Patterson.

Remember, never visit a cemetery after dark and never visit alone.

~~~~~

Maria Deyo's House

(Springtown Road)

Throughout history reports of infanticide have always shocked people. How could a parent, particularly a mother, kill her own child? The idea that a mother could do such a thing—after all, a mother is supposed to support and nurture her children—horrifies us as we try to understand the reasons something like this could happen. More often than not, in cases of maternal infanticide we are left with more questions than answers. This was the case in 1801 in New Paltz.

According the "An Elegy on the Death of Maria Deyo" by Samuel S. Freer, the morning of September 13, 1801 started out like every other day for the Deyo family...except Maria Deyo seemed particularly eager to get on with her household chores. Giving no indication of her plans or intent, she hurried her husband out to his farm chores and her eldest son she sent off on an errand. Once alone with her three youngest children, she instructed her son to go off and play. She took her daughter into a back room and using a sharp knife slit her throat from ear to ear. Once finished, she called for the boy she had sent out to play. She also slit the boy's throat from ear to ear. Her eldest, who she had sent on an errand, must have sensed that something wasn't right because, instead of going on his errand, he had stayed on the farm. He heard the murderous sounds coming from the house. He returned to the house to find his brother's throat slit and him lying in a pool of blood. The younger boy, bleeding

Maria Deyo's House, New Paltz... Maria Deyo slit the throats of her three small children before killing herself.

from the throat, had tried to flee, but collapsed on the floor just inside the door. Maria then killed her infant, also by slitting the baby's throat, and finally herself. Her husband, alerted by his oldest son, rushed to the house to find the house filled with blood, gore, and the dead bodies of his wife and three youngest children.

The horrific news spread fast throughout the area. Samuel S. Freer, publisher of the *Ulster County Gazette*, was moved to write elegy of Maria and her children. I have no doubt that this news made the front page of the paper and sold many copies.

In the poem, Freer writes "a ghost was seen" and "A spectre there appears—/With reeking blade and bloody hand." While Samuel Freer may have made the reference to ghosts and spectres for poetic effect, there is a good chance that after such a senseless and gory crime a haunting would appear. I have no doubt that if it isn't today, the house was haunted at one time. Very rarely do spirits who meet such a violent death at the hands of a loved one pass over peacefully.

Samuel Freer's Elegy

AN
ELEGY
ON THE DEATH
OF
MARIA DEYO
WHO PUT AN END TO THE EXISTENCE OF
HERSELF, AND THREE INFANT CHILDREN,
ON SUNDAY MORNING
THE 13TH OF SEPTEMBER 1801
WITH REMARKS AND PROSE ON THE HORRID
CRIME OF
SUICIDE

"Alas! It was a piteous deed"

KINGSTON, (Ulster County) PRINTED
BY SAMUEL S. FREER
1801

ELEGY

AH! listen to the cruel talk,
Of horror, grief, and woe;
No ballad does the like unfold:
No age the like can shew

Amidst the woods near Hurley Town
This tragic scene took place;
I cannot half describe its parts—
The outlines I may trace.

The wife of one Deyo, (by name)
To all the virtues dear,
Liv'd free from imputation bare,
As far as we can hear.

Her husband tenderly she lov'd—
In paths of peace they trod:
The sweetest union grac'd their lives
And cheer'd their lone abode.

The grove was still & nature smil'd:
In church the prayer was heard,
When quick she form'd her murd'rous plan
And God no longer fear'd.

That morn, intent on house affairs,
How wond'rous strange to say,
She advised some of her family
To leave the house straightway

The husband she inclin'd to go
To view the fields of grain:
And elder son she sent from home,
That she her end might gain.

A son and daughter yet remain'd
Destin'd to tragic fate.
Of tender years caress'd by her,
No objects of her hate.

A razor sharp she had prepar'd,
the instrument of blood,
She tells the boy to go to play,
As near her then he stood.

Swift he obeys with heart of joy,
Unconscious of her scheme.
She calls the little girl to her__
The little girls she came.

In chamber dark, fit for the deed,
She then the child conveyed,
Stuck with the frenzy of her eyes,
It loudly sobbed and pray'd—

Ah! mother! mother! don't it cries,
Ah, mother dear, forbear!
Unmov'd she hears it piteous tone—
She cuts from ear to ear!!

Her dark design not yet fulfill'd
She calls her son from play,
She seizes fast the murd'rous blade
To take his life away.

The son she sent upon an errand,
Had tarried near the place,
He heard a cry—a dying groan,--
the cause he could not trace.

The other struggling for his life,
He drapes her bloody arm—
He sees his red—his mangl'd throat,
He runs with sad alarm.

He sees him fall upon the earth,
he hears his dying moan—
While from the mansion forth there came
A deeper parting groan.

For next, the reeking blade she grasp'd
No dying word she made—
She strikes—the stream of gore does rush,
What horror is display'd.

More cruel than the wolves or bears,
Her helpless babe she kills,
By fatal train of mental thought
Their youthful blood she spills.

Ah! who can paint the husband's looks,
His agony and woe:
Frantick he comes to view the scene,
And wanders to and fro.

He sees his wife—his children dear,
Lie weltering in their gore;
He calls to them—no voice returns
To life they wake no more.

How dread and frightful was that night,
The screech owl hooted shrill—
A light appear'd—a ghost was seen—
These sights the blood did chill.

Loud moans assail the list'ning ear
Lamenting their sad doom—
The bat it flits and terrifies,
And awful in the gloom,

In the earth she lies entomb'd
A spectre there appears—
With reeking blade and bloody hand,
And awful form it wears.

O Christ have mercy on her soul,
and rescue it from hell,
Without thy aid in endless fire,
Forever it must dwell.

Reader! 'tis thine to wait the will
Of him who gave you life.
'Tis thine to conquer erring pride,
And calm the passion's strife.

Better t bear those ills we have'—
Our necessary pain—
Than fly to those we know not of'—
And misery our gain.

Few and transient are the days
The soul remains in clay;
Tis yours to act a Christian's part
Till death takes you away.

~~~

Visiting the Deyo House

† Springtown Road runs from New Paltz, just off Route 299 to Tillson. You may also get to Springtown Road from Tillson by taking River Road and turning left onto Springtown Road. There are two stone houses on Springtown Road; one is marked with a historic marker, the other is not. The stone house without the marker is the Maria Deyo house. The Deyo house is covered with white stucco and does not have exposed stones. This covering was the way the houses were originally. Please remember this is private property. Do not trespass.

~~~~~~~

Chapter Twenty-Seven:

Napanoch

Shanley Hotel

Though Shanley Hotel is not in the Hudson Valley, it is definitely worth the detour. The hotel, located on the corner of Main and Clinton Streets in Napanoch, was originally built in 1845. It is considered one of the most haunted places in the United States.

The Shanley Hotel had several owners and names throughout its history, but it now bears the name of James Louis Shanley, who purchased the hotel in 1906. Shanley was a rich and famous businessman before he purchased the hotel. Eleanor Roosevelt and Thomas Edison were reportedly friends of his and are said to have spent time visiting him in the hotel in Napanoch.

Shanley Hotel, Ellenville... One of the most haunted places in the United States. The hotel boasts of ghosts 24/7.

The hotel is the site of many tragic deaths and mysterious happenings: the Shanleys lost all three of their children within nine months of their births; the young daughter of the hotel's barber died from a fall into a well across the street; and a man named Joe supposedly killed his girlfriend in one of the upstairs rooms. In addition, the hotel sports hidden rooms and passage used to hide booze during prohibition and perhaps even some more nefarious and sinister usages.

James Shanley died in 1937, which started the decline of the hotel. It was used as a rooming house and eventually was slated to be converted into modern apartments. However, Salvatore and Cynthia Nicosia purchased the hotel to save its history and are now painstakingly restoring the hotel to its former glory.

The hotel is open for ghost hunts. I have talked with a few people who have visited the Shanley and they have reported hearing music, voices, and singing...as if a party was going on. They also report feelings of being touched or their hair being pulled. One woman showed me photos of orbs. She also claimed to have seen a shadowy figure in the upstairs hallway. Some people claim to feel an overwhelming sense of heaviness in their chest in certain areas of the hotel.

According to the Shanley's website, ghostly activity can be experienced twenty-four hours a day: there is the ghost of Emma cooking meals; sounds of *spirit* guests; and even James Shanley still wanders about, whistling and opening doors. A piano can also be heard playing ragtime music and happy children can be heard all over the hotel.

"Through out the day and evenings, rocking chairs can be seen rocking on their own, mysterious clocks chime, cold and hot spots felt, along with unfamiliar smells. Some have seen an aberration and feelings of being watched and followed. Many guest have witnessed objects balancing in an unusual position or jewelry being pulled off. Seemingly, "the good old boys" have a great sense of humor! Listen in silence; one can hear dance music, the chatter of voices, laughter or encounter hair raising moans.

The Shanley Hotel consists of 35 rooms, hidden basements, secret pathways and the seductive "Bordello." Upon entering the Bordello, people have reported feeling light-headed, shortness of breath, heaviness and an over-whelming feeling of joy/sadness. A photo has been also taken of a 'Young Lady' star-gazing towards the mountains from a window. Therefore, the 'Bordello' is considered the most active place in the Hotel!"

http://www.shanleyhotel.com/

Since the hotel actively holds ghost hunts, psychic readings, and séances, it will most likely remain haunted since it is retaining its old haunted energy and gaining some new.

Visiting the Shanley Hotel

† Shanley Hotel, P.O. Box 394, Napanoch, New York 12458
Website: www.shanleyhotel.com
Proprietor: Cynthia Nicosia,
845-210-4267, cindy@shanleyhotel.com
Proprietor: Salvatore Nicosia,
845-467-7056, sal@shanleyhotel.com

Chapter Twenty-Eight:

Ellenville

Potterville

Founded by Potter family in the late 1800s, Potterville was a hamlet outside of Ellenville, New York, that, today, no longer exists. The Potters had a large mill and employed several families to help run the mill. In the early 1900s, the mill burned to the ground. The Potters decided not to rebuild and moved out of the area. This started the exodus of the other families from the area. However, according to legend, one night, in one of the few remaining families, a father shot his entire family and then killed himself. The grand finale came for Potterville when the only bridge to the hamlet washed out in the 1920s and the town decided not to rebuild. Up until 2002, several buildings still existed in Potterville. When New York

The road to Potterville, Ellenville... Potterville is the former site of an abandoned village filled with ghostly presences.

State took over the land, the buildings were torn down for safety reasons. However, it's easy to discern, based on domestic plants, such as lilacs and lilies, as well as stonewalls, where the houses stood.

Once you cross the stream *(sorry, no bridge, you'll have to wade)*, you will immediately feel the energy here. People have claimed to see shadow-like figures walking on the roadway, hearing indistinct voices, and seeing orbs of light. This is a great spot to collect EVPs. There are many clear ghostly energies in this spot. When I arrived in the area known as Potterville, the scent flowers filled the entire area with a strong beautiful smell. Though there were a few flowering bushes, such as lilac, there were not enough flowering trees to account for the strong scent of flowers I could smell. As soon as I crossed the stream, I felt like I was in a very magical, or, at least, energetic place.

The site of the former village is accessible only by foot. It is not a difficult hike; the road, though rutted, is mostly flat. Wear good hiking shoes. You will drive down Lundy Road as far as your car can make it. The road is only maintained as far as the Lundy estate. From the Lundy Estate to Potterville is approximately a mile. Drive past the Lundy estate and park on the side of the road. Remember, the Lundy estate is a private residence and has security. Do not trespass. Do not block the road, as four-wheelers, bikers, and brave souls do try to use the road. As you drive down Lundy Road to Potterville and later, as you walk to Potterville, you will find evidence of the past on both sides of the roads. You will see an abandoned Dutch stone house, now owned by the State of New York. You'll see the remains of a mill dam, stone walls, old foundations, and even a few road signs. Do not forget to keep snapping pictures. This is truly a "ghost town" experience... one the entire family can really enjoy.

I have a couple of words of warning before visiting Potterville. The first warning is to use insect repellant. The entire area is posted with tick warnings. Even using good repellant, I still brought home several ticks. For this reason, I strongly recommend you do not bring pets. In addition, I strongly suggest that the ONLY souvenirs you take from this site are pictures and EVPs. The area on the far side of the river, Potterville Proper, is said to contain such haunted energies, people have reported strange noises and rappings after bringing "artifacts" home. It is tempting to bring home a souvenir, but everything is best left where it is found. Also, while it is tempting to visit Potterville at night, if you must, make sure you have enough batteries for flashlights. It is very, very dark there at night. The Potterville Proper Village site is owned by New York State; therefore the land is open for public visit, day or night. Be forewarned that some young people do use the area as a "Lover's Lane," so it's best to visit in the day.

Potterville... The author's daughter stands in what is left of the Potterville Bridge washout.

Visiting Potterville

† Take Lundy Road off of Route 209 just outside of Ellenville. It will eventually turn into a dirt road. While traveling down Lundy Road, there will be several places you may want to stop and take pictures such as the old mill dam and the stone house. The stone house is posted, but I was able to get some interesting photos from the roadside.

† Walk about a mile straight down the road. Keep your eyes and ears open. Ghosts abound. You will have to wade across the stream to get to Potterville. Please choose a shallow area to wade. If there has been heavy rains and the streams seems impassable, postpone your visit to another time. Remember, those remnants of the bridge you see were washed out by a spring flood. Water is a very formidable force. Once in Potterville only follow the road as far as it is discernable. I recommend you go no further. You do not want to get lost in the woods. Stay in a group.

† Another suggestion is to visit in the late spring or early fall. Do not visit after a rain, as the road will be muddy and the stream will be difficult to cross. Do not visit Potterville alone. It's a good place to plan a day hike with family or friends. Bring water. You will not want to drink out of the stream. Freshwater streams can hold viruses, bacteria and parasites. This was one of the most delightfully haunted places I have visited. I'm sure you'll enjoy it as well.

Chapter Twenty-Nine:

Kingston, New York

Rondout Light House

The Rondout Lighthouse is located in the Hudson River just off Kingston Point Landing in Kingston at the mouth of the Rondout Creek. It is the third lighthouse built in at this location. This lighthouse was originally lit in 1915 to guide boats up and down the Hudson River. The lighthouse was occupied by the keeper and his family until 1946. In 1984, the Hudson Maritime Museum took over the care and maintenance of the lighthouse. In 2002, the ownership of the lighthouse was transferred to the City of Kingston.

I spoke with a volunteer who helped clean and maintain the lighthouse years ago. Since the lighthouse is easy access from passing boats, the lighthouse was padlocked from the outside each night to keep it safe and secure from break-ins. The volunteer would arrive well before the lighthouse was opened to the public several times a week to clean it. Each cleaning day, when she arrived, she would find an "impression" as if someone had slept on top of the one of the beds. She said she would always find clumps of mud as if they had fallen off someone's shoe onto the floor even though the lighthouse is surrounded by a concrete landing.

However, she became convinced that earlier lighthouse keepers were still there watching over the boats that still sail up and down the Hudson. One day while putting a small vacuum away under a bed, she heard a clinking noise. Looking under the bed, she found a small chamber pot, one like a child might use. She was surprised to find some coins in the pot. She put them in her pocket and thought nothing of it. However, the next day, when she pulled the chamber pot out from under the bed, there were coins in it. Every time, after that, when she went to the house, she always found a few coins in the chamber pot. She asked all the volunteers about it and none seemed to be able to shed any light as to who was putting coins in the pot. Actually, besides herself, no one had even known there was a chamber pot tucked under the bed. She decided the spirits wanted the coins there and she stopped taking them out.

She also told me that she and other volunteers have heard the sound of footsteps on the stairs. Old lighthouse keepers took their jobs very seriously, since lives depended on them. This volunteer strongly believes that one of the old lighthouse keepers are still around making sure nothing goes wrong.

Visiting the Rondout Lighthouse

† Hudson River Maritime Museum, 50 Rondout Landing, Kingston, NY 12401
Website: www.hrmm.org
Phone: 845-338-0071

Trips to the Rondout Lighthouse are available through the Hudson River Maritime Museum. The Museum is open May through October. Trips out to the lighthouse are by reservation only and held on the first Saturday of each month, June through October. There is a fee to visit the lighthouse. Please call in advance.

~~~~~

Montrepose Cemetery

Montrepose Cemetery is a delightfully Victorian cemetery. If you love Victorian charm, you will love this cemetery. Montrepose is a visual treat. The front wrought iron gates are a truly work of art. Many famous people are buried in this cemetery: Thomas Cornell, United States Congressman from New York, 1867-1869; Anton Otto Fischer, famous illustrator for the *Saturday Evening Post*; Arthur Sherwood Flemming, United States Secretary of Health, Education and Welfare, 1958–1961; James Girard Lindsley, Mayor of Kingston in 1872 and Unites States Representative from New York, 1885-1887; Jervis McEntee, Hudson River School Artist and brother-in-law of Calvert Vaux; and Calvert Vaux, himself, a building and landscape architect. Vaux designed the Hoyt's Mansion (The Point), Wilderstein and the grounds of the Mid-Hudson Psychiatric Center.

As most people know when the circumstances of a person's death are mysterious it often creates restless spirits. For this reason, the ghost of Calvert Vaux is thought to haunt Montrepose. Calvert Vaux's death have always remained rather mysterious. On November 19, 1895, Calvert Vaux was visiting his son in Brooklyn. He went out for a walk but did not return. His body was later found in Graveshead Bay. Though his death was ruled accidental, many believed that Calvert Vaux committed suicide. To add to the tragedy of the Vaux family, Calvert's daughter, Helen Donaldson, committed suicide by hanging herself in the basement of her home on November 10, 1904. Calvert's son, Downing, was killed in an accidental fall from a roof on May 15, 1926, though also thought to be a possible suicide. Vaux is seen standing next to his grave and other nearby areas, as if in contemplation. Vaux appears as he did in life, in a long coat and

Montrepose Cemetery, Kingston... Montrepose is known for its glowing orbs of light.

has bushy hair and spectacles. He will dissipate slowly once noticed. One witness told me that if you do not look directly at Vaux he will remain.

In the graveyard, the Coykendall (pronounced KIRK-en-dahl) family has a large, park-like memorial that covers over 2.5 acres of the cemetery. The Coykendall's were a wealthy family, involved in many in many local industries; banking, railroads, and mining. The monument has a long pathway and is beautiful to visit. Unfortunately, it is falling into disrepair. There are no upright gravestones, rather there are in ground memorial stones and a large mausoleum in the center of a stone arbor. There is also plenty of evidence of vandalism. However, you can still enjoy the this monument. You can sit on its benches and take pictures of other parts of this cemetery.

Over in the corner, way in the back of this cemetery is a separate, gated Jewish cemetery dating from the late nineteenth and early twentieth cemetery. It's worth visiting this area. Traditionally, when you visit a Jewish grave you leave a small stone or pebble. In respect of those whose graves I visit or photograph, I always leave a stone.

All of Montrepose Cemetery, like most cemeteries is haunted. People have claimed to see ghost like figures towards dusk and strange, unexplainable orbs of light. As part of my work, I visit many cemeteries. I enjoy visiting cemeteries and find them very peaceful and relaxing. Montrepose is one of the rare exceptions. This cemetery made me feel "uneasy." It has nothing to do with the look of the cemetery. It is very scenic and has tree lined drives. Take plenty of pictures. I'm sure you will get an orb or a mist shot in this cemetery. Remember to always observe cemetery etiquette and, like most cemeteries, this one closes at dusk. Do not trespass—and *never* visit a cemetery alone.

Visiting Montrepose Cemetery

† Montrepose Cemetery, 75 Montrepose Avenue, Kingston, New York 12401.
Phone: 845-331-0592
Website: www.interment.net/data/us/ny/ulster/montrepose/html

From Broadway, turn up West Chester Street. The cemetery is at the corner of West Chester Street and Montrepose Avenue and is open dawn until dusk.

~~~~~

Old Stockade Area

Kingston was a "walled city." The Dutch immigrants and the local Native American engaged in skirmishes about land rights. As a result, the Colonial Governor, Peter Stuyvesant, ordered a wall to be erected around the settlement, at that time consisting of about fifty families. A fourteen-foot wooden wall, constructed of tree trunks was erected. This walled city was called Wiltwyck by the Dutch, later to be renamed Kingston. In 1971, part of the original wall was found along Clinton Avenue. Even though the wall is gone, the streets of the original Wyltwick are laid out as they were in 1658. When you walk in this area, you truly walking on very historic ground.

On October 17, 1777, British troops entered the city and burned over three hundred homes and buildings. This event is known locally as "The Burning of Kingston." There are a great many heroic stories that come from this event. Even though the city was burned, twenty-one pre-Revolutionary homes are still standing in the Stockade Area, a wonderful tribute to the early Dutch homebuilders. All of the homes in the area are privately owned but a walking tour is available. The entire "stockade area" as it is known today, is well haunted by earlier settlers, survivors of the burning of Kingston, as well a full array ghosts from all eras of Kingston's early history. A local Kingston historian told me that there are as probably as many ghosts as people in the Stockade Area!

Once you are familiar with the Stockade Area, you can visit this area anytime to ghost hunt. However, you should take care walking after dark. Do not travel alone.

Visiting the Old Stockade

† Friends of Historic Kingston Museum, Historic Kingston Museum, Wall and Main Streets
  Phone 845-339-0720
  Website: www.fohk.org

The Friends of Historic Kingston offer a two-hour tour on Saturdays from May through October, departing at 2 p.m. from the Friends of Historic Kingston Museum, corner of Wall and Main Streets.

~~~~~

Old Dutch Reformed Church and Cemetery

Even if you weren't looking for ghosts, The First Reformed Protestant Dutch Church, or it's local name "The Old Dutch Church" is a visual and historic treat to visit. It is located at the corner of Wall Street and Main Street in Kingston in the center of the Stockade district of Kingston. This is one area of the Mid-Hudson Valley where you could encounter a ghost at any moment; it is so rich in history and haunting.

The church was founded in 1659. The current structure is the third church to be built on this site. The second stone church was burned on October 17, 1777 during the "Burning of Kingston" by the British during the Revolutionary War. This left the structure gutted. The current structure was finished and dedicated in 1852.

The church steeple is haunted and has been haunted from pre-Revolutionary days. In the early 1700s the church pastor and his wife were on the Hudson River traveling home from a long journey. A storm kicked up and the crew feared an evil spirit had invaded the ship. Unable to steer the ship, the terrified crew and passengers begged the minister to pray. He performed an exorcism and the ship arrived safely in Kingston. However, much to the minister's horror, he found a hat of what he believed was the evil spirit, or hobgoblin, in the church steeple when he arrived safely home. How the hobgoblin got there no one knew, but as long as the church and surrounding land remained hallowed, the evil spirit was trapped in the steeple. His ghostly moaning can be heard on stormy nights. Flashes of his grotesque face can be seen during lightening storms.

Old Dutch Church, Kingston... The steeple of this church is haunted by a hobgoblin.

In the 1850s a painter is said to have died in the steeple while repainting it. Many believe the evil spirit had appeared to him and scared him to death. Claims have been made that the painter can still be seen working diligently up on the steeple on nights with a full moon. On December 24, 1853 the steeple blew down in a terrible storm. Many say it was the spirit trying to release itself from the newly erected church. The church had to close for ten months for renovations.

The evil spirit is also credited with changing the XII to XIII in the steeple clock on the Wall Street side of the steeple clock. If you look up you can see the corrected "mistake."

Surrounding the church is the haunted churchyard. The graves in this churchyard date back as into the 1600s. However, the oldest dated stone is 1710. It is important to note that not every burial was marked with a tombstone. There are more bodies underground then there are stone above ground.

You will find stones marked with an "X," known as a St. Andrew's Cross. These mark the graves that were originally underneath the church but were moved out into the graveyard in 1883 during renovations. You'll find the classic tombstone design of the early American colonists, the unsettling skull with wings emerging from the back of its head. Reposing here is New York

State's first governor, George Clinton. It won't be hard to find his grave. It is the largest grave in the yard and lit at night. Along with being New York's first governor, he was also a Brigadier General in the Revolutionary War, and Vice President under Thomas Jefferson and James Madison. Clinton sighting have been reported around Kingston and here is one way to get a glimpse at the former governor in ghostly form. The graveyard is only open in daylight hours, however, since it boarders the sidewalk, you are welcome to walk around it at dusk, the best time to spot the shadowy figures said to walk among the graves.

Visiting the Olde Dutch Church and Churchyard

† Olde Dutch Church, 272 Wall Street Kingston, New York, 12401.
Phone 845-338-6759.
Website: www.olddutchchurch.org

Parking is metered on the streets. It's important to note when visiting the Old Dutch Church is that it is an active church, not a museum. While the grounds are open from dawn until dusk the church itself is not open to the public although you are welcome to join the congregants at worship.

~~~~~

Senate House

During the Revolutionary War, the New York State government, still in its formative stage, had no regular place to meet. These brave politicians were literally being chased up the Hudson River by the British. As a result, the Senate moved ever northwards, finding new places that it could meet. The Senate House, located in Kingston, New York, was one of the earliest places that the New York State Senate met. In September and October of 1777, the Senate met in the stone house of Abraham Van Gaasbeek, a merchant.

The beautiful Dutch stone house was built in the 1680s, almost a century before the Senate met there. Wessel Ten Broeck, descendant of one of the founding families of Kingston, owned this home until it was sold to the State of New York in 1887. A two story museum was added next to the Senate house in 1927 and now holds a treasure trove of early American art and artifacts.

Though Aaron Burr was not a member of this original senate, he is said to have visited the house as a guest in the small tavern run in the house.

Senate House, Kingston... The faint strains of the violin of a lovesick girl can be heard playing for Aaron Burr.

As a young girl, Sarah Van Gaasbeek was said to have had fallen in love with Aaron Burr. Each time she saw Burr, she would shyly play her violin for him in hopes of gaining his affection. Unfortunately, Sarah contracted an illness and died when she was still a very young girl. Since she associated her violin with her love of Burr she did not want anyone else to hear it played. She begged her father to wall up the violin in the house so it could never be found and played again. Some residents of Kingston still say that if you stay at the Senate House overnight, you hear the faint sound of Sarah playing her violin for Burr.

I have visited the house many times and volunteer and tour guides have told me that besides Sarah's violin there are reports of foot steps and doors unlatching themselves and the glimpse of figures out of the corner of their eye.

Visiting the Senate House

> † Senate House State Historic Site, 296 Fair Street, Kingston, New York 12401
> Phone: 845-338-2786
> Website: http://nysparks.state.ny.us/

The site is only open seasonally for tours, though you may tour the grounds at any time of the year. Parking is located directly across from the Senate House and is free.

Chapter Thirty:

Athens

Athens Light House... Near this lighthouse the wreck of the *Swallow* occurred. Dozens of people were drowned in the freezing waters.

Do you want to visit a place that will make you feel like you have stepped backwards in time? Then Athens is the place you want to visit! I find myself coming back to this town because I find it so delightful and the spirits are always so welcoming. Athens is a sleepy little village located on the Hudson River. In it's heyday it was a busy ferry port for the Hudson River, as well as, a thriving boat-building community. Now the town lies quiet on the banks of the Hudson. Athens has over three hundred historic buildings and a walk through Athens is a treat for those interested in nineteenth century architecture. Along with the beautiful homes, many spirits who wander through this quaint, historic town.

As peaceful as Athens is, it has some unlikely claims to fame. In its earlier history there was a terrible crash just off the shore of the steamship *The Swallow*. This crash was made famous in 1845 in a lithograph by Currier and Ives. More recently, in 2004, Athens was one of several sites used in the production of Steven Spielberg's *War of the Worlds* starring Tom Cruise and Dakota Fanning

~~~~~

Trinity Episcopal Church

When the Trinity Episcopal Church was founded, there was no building and the members first met in the schoolhouse. John G. Voogd was a slave owner and a wealthy member of Trinity Church. Upon his death, Voogd left his estate to the church for the express purpose of building a new church building. Voogd's will stipulated that his remains should be interred under the pulpit of the church to be erected. There seems to be some disagreement as to whether Voogd's remains were simply interred under the altar or under the actual pulpit itself. In 1853, according to church records, Voogd was re-interred in the church and a plaque was hung in the vestry in memory of John G. Voogd.

As the membership grew, a new church was built in the village and the old church was sold. Voogd remains were removed from the church and buried in the Mt Hope Cemetery. You can move the body but you can't make the spirit move with it! John Voogd still haunts North Montgomery Street, wondering why his wishes are not carried out. Voogd can be seen at the site of the original church, walking the grounds or standing under the trees.

~~~~~

The Steamship The Swallow

Steamboating was born on the Hudson River. Robert Fulton first steamed up the Hudson from New York to Albany on August 14, 1807. A steamboat was a quick and reliable way to navigate the Hudson. Also, steamboating was an elegant way to travel, allowing passengers to have a leisurely passage and arriving rested at their destination. Soon steamboats were the most popular way of traversing the great river.

On April 7, 1845, *The Swallow* was on its way to New York City. A late spring snowstorm made sailing unpleasant and visibility low. However, it did not stop the *The Swallow* from racing two other steamships, *The Express* and *The Rochester,* both also headed for New York City. Though racing was an unsafe practice, it was common among steamboat captains.

As *The Swallow* was approaching Athens's west channel the boat struck Droopers Island, seriously damaging the ship. (Droopers Island no longer exists in the Hudson, it was blasted out of the channel.) Flames erupted and only a small portion of deck remained above waters. People were forced into the cold waters of the Hudson River. Residents of Athens scrambled on to small boats rowing frantically to save the passengers in water. The other steamboats navigated the dangerous channel in an attempt to save lives.

Accurate passenger logs were not kept aboard steamships and the loss of life could only be estimated. Estimates range that from forty to over one hundred passengers lost their lives on the stormy Hudson that evening.

When an April snowstorm strikes on the banks of the Hudson, the scene of the accident is said to briefly replay itself. Flames can be seen shooting up in the falling snow and passengers can be heard crying for help. Small boats can be seen battling the waves in effort to save lives. The two large steamboats can be seen navigating the treacherous waters in an attempt to save the passengers of *The Swallow*. Shocked observers claim the scene fades as fast as it seemingly appeared leaving them standing alone on the quiet banks of the snowy Hudson.

~~~~~

Murderers Creek

Murderers Creek runs into the Hudson River just north of the village of Athens. The creek is named for the unsolved murder of a young Village woman. The ghost of this murder victim still walks the shore. Sometime in the early-late 1700s, Sally Hamilton, was visiting neighbors. Not wanting to be out after dark, Sally hurried to return home as dusk began to fall. Her house was just a short distance from her neighbor's. At home, as the skies were darkening, her family began to grow worried. It was unlike Sally to be out after dark. Her father sent a family member to ask why Sally had not come home, but the nieghbor claimed she had left for home quite awhile before. Alarmed, the family began to look for her at other neighbors' homes, but no one had seen Sally. The family quickly formed a small search party of family and concerned neighbors and began to look for the young woman. One of the neighbors claimed that earlier in the evening he had heard the sounds of someone crying out, but had originally thought it just was children at play or the wind.

The next morning Sally's body was found floating in the creek and it has been called Murderers Creek ever since. A man named Kavanaugh was arrested and tried for the crime, but he was acquitted due to lack of evidence. The local residents, believing in their own justice, drove him out of town. Later, a man named Lent confessed to the crime. Lent claimed he and his friend, Sickler, had accosted the girl on her way home. However,

Bridge at Murderers Creek, Athens... The ghost of Sally Hamilton, a young woman who was murdered on the shores of this creek, is seen walking and weeping near here.

their confession was to save them from being shot as deserters from the Army! Their superior officers swore that both men were in their barracks, fifty miles away on the night of the murder. Lent was sent to prison for perjury and Sickler was acquitted of any wrongdoing.

There was no justice for Sally Hamilton. Her killer was never caught. Sally is said to haunt the creek. Sightings of Sally are reported along the banks of the creek near Athens. She carries a basket and appears to be crying. Some people have reported hearing her sobs. Other times, she will stand silently, staring sadly into the observer's eyes before she disappears.

Visiting Athens

† Athens is located on Route 385, off Route 9W. Don't miss the village. It is easy to do since a new road was built as a by pass. You can park at the waterfront and enjoy walking around this wonderful village.

† Murderers Creek runs under Route 385 just north of the village. There is a public boat launch area where the creek meets the Hudson. You can park in this area. The creek is clearly marked.

† The Old Trinity Church was located on North Montgomery Street.

Chapter Thirty-One:

Leeds

Salisbury Manor

Ghosts of those who have been murdered and have not received justice seem to be some of the most persistent hauntings. One of the most terrifying ghostly sightings in the Hudson Valley is based on a gruesome murder in Leeds. In the late 1700s, a man named William Salisbury had a servant named Anna Dorthea Swarts. Anna was said to be a young, spirited girl in contrast to her master's solitary, serious manner. William Salisbury was one of the richest men in town but he was also said to be a cruel and unkind man. He worked Anna mercilessly and beat her for the slightest infraction. In 1755, in a blind rage, Salisbury tied Anna to his horse and she was dragged to death. Her offense wasn't clear. Some say she had

Salisbury Manor, Leeds... Anna Dorthea Swarts was tied to the back of a horse and dragged to her death near this spot. Her ghostly form still wanders the area.

gotten pregnant, others say she had tried to run away from her tyrannical owner and had been caught. Salisbury was arrested and brought before the jury for indictment. In 1762, the court decided that they could not determine if the death of Anna was premeditated murder or an accident. Some say Salisbury claimed he had only tied Anna to the horse so she would not run away and the horse "spooked" accidentally dragging Anna to her death accidentally. Others say William tied the girl to the horse and then whipped the horse so it would run away. Did William Salisbury get away with murdering a young innocent girl?

The indictment against William Salisbury reads:

> The Jurors for our Lord the King, for the body of the County of Albany, upon their Oath do Present: That William Salisbury of Katskill in the County of Albany Yeoman, on the twenty sixth day of May in the twenty-eight year of the Reign of our late Sovereign Lord King George the second, with force and arms [illegible]kill aforesaid in the county aforesaid in and upon Anna Dorthea Swarts, then serving the said William Salisbury in his Service at the Katskill aforesaid retained, did make an assault and the body of her the said Anna Dorthea Swarts then and there with a certain cord did bind about and the said Anna Dorothea Swarts so being bound to the tail of a certain horse of him the said William Salisbury of the value of three pounds then and there with the same cord did bind and tye and the said horse then and there with force and arms did beat and force and compel the aforesaid horse so swiftly to run that the horse aforesaid the aforesaid Anna Dorothea Swarts upon her body did strike of which the said Anna Dorothea Swarts then and there instantly died. And so the jurors aforesaid upon their oath aforesaid do say that the said William Salisbury the said Anna Dorothea Swarts then and there I the manner and form aforesaid, feloniously, willfully and of his malice aforethought did kill and murder against the peace of our said late Lord the King his crown and dignity.

On the reverse side of the judgment, jury foreman Abraham [illegibly] signs simply *"Ignoramus,"* which is Latin for "we do not know." Why did it take seven years after the death of Anna for Salisbury to face a jury? Why was he brought up in front of the court in the first place will never be known. Was there a witness to the gruesome crime? Was William Salisbury freed because the incident was truly was an accident? Was there lack of evidence? Or was Salisbury freed because he was a rich and influential man? We'll never know. But what we do know is that the troubled spirit of Anna still haunts Leeds.

After such a short and troubled life Anna's spirit could not rest. Almost immediately, people started to see strange and terrifying apparitions where

Anna was dragged to her death. A huge white horse, nostrils flaring and eyes in a panic is seen galloping at full speed dragging behind it the body of Anna in tattered rags. Anna can be heard screaming for help as the image disappears. Images of Anna as a walking skeleton have also been reported. The oddest reported image is Anna, sitting on a large boulder next to the side of the road in tattered clothes. Each one of her fingers is lighted as if each is a candle. Her eyes have no irises or pupils and appear pure white. She turns to the observer, fingers lit and splayed widely before she disappears.

Just as eerie as the specter that appears are the uncanny sounds people often report hearing at the scene of her grisly murder; a galloping snorting horse, horrifying screams, and loud sighs and moans. It seems that Annie's spirit cannot rest.

Visiting Salisbury Manor

† Salisbury Manor, Route 23B, Leeds, New York
Though designated as a historic landmark, Salisbury Manor is a private residence. Do not trespass. The house is located just outside the village. You can't miss it.

Chapter Thirty-Two:

Coxsackie

Village of Coxsackie

Coxsackie (cook-SACK-ee), New York, is a small village located on the west side of the Hudson River about half way between Kingston and Albany. Its odd name is derived from a mix of Native American and Dutch and is believed to mean "owl's hoot."

In colonial times, an old trapper lived near the river. He worked the land, lived alone and for the most part got along with the Native Americans who he traded with quite frequently. On one of his trading trips to a Native village, he spotted a lovely young Native American maiden and fell instantly in love with her. He began to visit the village frequently, wooing both her and her father's consent. She fell in love with the trapper and her father finally consented to the marriage.

Little did they both know that a local Brave had also fallen in love with the maiden. He had watched the on-going courtship with growing anger and jealously. On the night of the wedding, while the maiden and her new husband were headed home, the Brave attacked the old trapper. But the trapper's dog leapt at the Brave's throat. The trapper was able to disarm his attacker and humiliate the Brave with a sound beating.

The trapper and his new bride moved into the trapper's cabin and lived in wedded bliss. Soon, they had a new addition to their happy family. However, the jealous Brave never forgot how the trapper had stolen his woman and humiliated him. He planned a vicious revenge.

One day, while the trapper was out checking his trap lines, the Brave broke into the home, raped and beat the young bride, and beheaded the infant. When the trapper returned home, his bride was so devastated it took the trapper three days to get the story from her. Finally, the young Native American woman succumbed to the heartbreak of losing her infant and died.

The trapper, blind with rage, traveled to the Native American village and demanded they turn over the Brave to him. They, too, were horrified of what had been done and willingly handed over the Brave for justice. Much to their surprise the trapper did not murder him on the spot, as expected. Instead, the trapper bound the Brave tightly, his arms to his side, threw a rope around his neck and led him off. Arriving back at his own cabin, he took the corpse of his bride and, horrifically, bound it, face-to-face with that of the Brave. With much labor, he secured both bodies to the back his horse. He then whipped the horse until it rode off into down to the banks of the Hudson dragging his dead bride and her murderer along behind him. The trapper himself disappeared and was never heard from again.

Legend says that the horse, laden with its two bodies still runs through the woods along the Hudson. Along with the horses hooves you can hear the Brave begging for his life. A ghostly imagine of a young Native American woman has been seen wandering the land down by the water, weeping, looking for her infant.

You can continue your ghost hunting along Coxsackie's waterfront. You'll want to visit the Reed Street Historic District. This is the oldest part of town, dating back to the land's purchase from the Native Americans in 1662. I have been told that this area of Coxsackie is haunted and a few people have reported shadowy and misty figures in the evening that disappear.

Visiting Coxsackie

† Take 385 into Coxsackie
Visit the Reed Street Historic District and Riverside Park

Afterword?

A short while ago, a few friends and I were dining on the patio of a restaurant in Kingston. It was late summer and there was the hint of a chill in the air. We sipped our drinks and glanced out at the reddening sunset. An unexpected wind came up and blew the napkins and several other items off our table. As we scrambled to retrieve the items, one of my friends said, "Do you think this place is haunted?" Placing the items back on the table, we all looked at each other. "I have my ghost bag in the car," I said. "I have a camera," one of my friends said. And ghost hunting can start as simply as that.

I am certainly not done visiting haunted places in the Hudson Valley or finding new ones. The river, the valleys, the mountains, villages, and forests all hold special energy here. Do you think a place is haunted? Go find out!

Bibliography

Adams, Arthur G. *The Hudson River Guidebook: A Guidebook to the River*. Albany, New York: State University of New York Press, 1981.

Bermpohl, Charles. "Even Stone Houses Have Haunts." *Kingston Daily Freeman*. October 31, 1968.

Carmer, Carl. *The Hudson*. New York, New York: Rinehart and Winston, 1974.

Daquino, Vincent T. *Hauntings of the Hudson Valley: An Investigative Journey*. Charleston, South Carolina: Haunted America, 2007.

Freer, Samuel. "Elegy on the Death of Maria Deyo." Transcribed photo copy of the original provided by Historic Huguenot Street Library and Archives.

Golan, Martin. "Area ghosts set for visits to favorite haunts." *Times Herald Record*. October 31, 1979.

Hauck, Dennis W. *The National Directory of Haunted Places*. New York, New York: Penguin Press, 1996.

Heidgerd, William. "Letter to Dr. Louis C. Jones." The New York State Historical Society. May 25, 1970.

Jones, Louis Clark. *Spooks of the Valley: Ghost Stories for Boys and Girls*. Eau Claire, Wisconsin: E.M. Hale and Co., 1965.

Ledwith, Miceal and Heinemann, Kaus. *The Orb Project*. New York, New York: Atria Books, 2007.

"Legends of Sinnipink." *New York Times*. August 19, 1894.

Macken, Linda Lee. *Haunted Houses of the Hudson Valley*. Ann Harbor, Michigan: Sherdian Books, 2006.

Mumford, Warren. "History: Danskammer Point Light." *Cornwall and Cornwall-on-Hudson*, 2007. Retrieved December 11 2008 at http://cornwall-on-hudson.com/article.cfm?page=718.

Palmer, John. "Ghost Stories from the Archives." *The Miscellany News*. October 28, 2005. Accessed from http://misc.vassar.edu/archives/2005/10/ghost_stories_f.html on December 2, 2007

Pritchard, Even T. *Native New Yorkers*. Tulsa, Oklahoma: Council Oak Books, 2002.

Reynolds, James. *Ghost in American Houses*. New York, New York: Farrar, Straus, and Cudahy, 1955.

Richardson, Judith. *Possessions: The History and Uses of Haunting in the Hudson Valley*. Cambridge, Massachusetts: Harvard University Press, 2005.

"Savages in Ulster County." *New Paltz Independent*. January 13, 1888.

Skinner, Charles, M. *Myths & Legends of Our Own Land*. Philadelphia, Pennsylvania: J.B. Lippincott Co., 1896.

William Salisbury's Indictment for murder. Photocopy of 1762 document from Green County Historical Society, Vedder Research Library.

Zimmerman, Linda. *Ghost Investigator*. Blooming Grove, New York: Spirited Publication, 2002.

Zimmerman, Linda. *Haunted Hudson Valley*. Piedmont, New York: Spirited Publication, 1999.

Index